SURRENDER, WHITE PEOPLE!

ALSO BY D.L. HUGHLEY

How Not to Get Shot

Black Man, White House

SURRENDER, WHITE PEOPLE!

OUR UNCONDITIONAL TERMS FOR PEACE

D.L. HUGHLEY

AND DOUG MOE

wm WILLIAM MORROW
An Imprint of HarperCollins*Publishers*

HarperCollins books may be purchased for educational, business, or sales promotional use. For information, please email the Special Markets Department at SPsales@harpercollins.com.

FIRST EDITION

Designed by Nancy Singer

Library of Congress Cataloging-in-Publication Data

Names: Hughley, D. L. (Darryl L.), 1963– author. | Moe, Doug, author.

Title: Surrender, white people! : our unconditional terms for peace / D. L. Hughley and Doug Moe.

Description: First edition. | New York : William Morrow, 2020.

Identifiers: LCCN 2020012324 (print) | LCCN 2020012325 (ebook) | ISBN 9780062953704 (hardcover) | ISBN 9780062953711 (trade paperback) | ISBN 9780062953728 (ebook)

Subjects: LCSH: United States—Race relations—Humor. | Whites—United States—Humor. | Race awareness—Humor. | African Americans—Humor.

Classification: LCC PN6231.R25 H84 2020 (print) | LCC PN6231.R25 (ebook) | DDC 305.89/6073—dc23

LC record available at https://lccn.loc.gov/2020012324

LC ebook record available at https://lccn.loc.gov/2020012325

ISBN 978-0-06-295370-4

20 21 22 23 24 LSC 10 9 8 7 6 5 4 3 2

To my father, Charles Hughley. I'll always try to make you proud.

CONTENTS

SURRENDER, WHITE PEOPLE!

SURRENDER, WHITE PEOPLE!

Surrender, white people! Time's up.

After four hundred years of oppression, discrimination, and bias, black folks are still here and we still won't shut the fuck up. And now we've got reinforcements. Just in my lifetime, the face of America has become a hell of a lot browner. In fact, we're on the cusp of being a majority-minority country. Let that sink in: whites will soon be a minority. This new reality carries consequences. White people have been in charge for a long time now, but black and brown folk are not going to take a back seat anymore. Whiteness ain't what it used to be. I'm here to say, it's time for white folks to sue for peace while the getting's still good.

Not that we won. No black or brown person can say "we won" with Trump in the White House or Tucker Carlson on the TV. Charlottesville, Botham Jean, and Atatiana Jefferson make it clear how far we still have to go. But the times *are* changing. As *The Atlantic* recently observed, "The United States is undergoing a transition perhaps no rich and stable democracy has ever experienced: Its historically dominant group is on its way to becoming a political minority— and its minority groups are asserting their co-equal rights and interests." Damn right.

So here we are. Nobody's winning, everybody's losing. We're all angry. We've been at it so long that it feels like we'll always have racial conflict and like we'll never figure out how to live together in peace and harmony. Whatever happened to ebony and ivory living side by side on my piano keyboard?

What we have here in America is a dysfunctional relationship. It's an unhappy marriage after a shotgun wedding. Oh, and after slavery, Jim Crow, and lynchings. So, ya know, we got issues.

But this country's not going to therapy, because America

doesn't want to deal with her issues. White people hate talking about race. "Why is everything about race?" they say. "Why do we always have to talk about race?" Everything's about race, because in America, it's *always* been about race here. The places we could work and live, the places we could eat, the places we could go to school.

It's the same today. How are we supposed to deal with Charlottesville if we don't know the same history? How are we supposed to trust the police if we don't acknowledge the continuing violence against us, as well as centuries of forced subjugation by white authorities? Where white people see an obsession with victimhood, black people see a willful lack of taking responsibility. When will white people let us be part of America?

Peace and reconciliation will only happen, I believe, when white people surrender their unjust privileges and their delusions of "supremacy." Look your history in the face, put aside all your visions of superiority, open up your institutions so they benefit everyone in this nation, and join the rest of us as equals. That's what I mean by surrender.

But America still has a white supremacy complex, still wants to bring black and brown people to heel. Slavery, Jim Crow, and segregation all tried to get black people to be like good little children, seen but not heard. Maybe not even seen.

And then you voted for Obama: "Fuck it, okay; I'll vote for a black guy this one time. Now this will make them shut up." But then we didn't shut up, so we got Trump as payback. Soon enough, African countries were "shitholes," brown people were in cages, and Nazis were marching in our streets.

So I'm going to solve our problems with this book. This book will do more for white people than the Obama election ever did. It'll do more than rooting for a black quarterback, more than celebrating Martin Luther King Jr. Day. You tried all these little things, hoping that we'd shut up, but it didn't quite get you there.

So fine, you don't want to hear from us anymore? This book is about how we can get black people to stop talking about oppression, discrimination, and our place in America. You give us this stuff and you get the niggers to shut the fuck up about it!

Surrender, white people! These are our terms:

WHY WE NEED A PEACE TREATY

A peace treaty, D.L.? Isn't that a bit . . . dramatic?

Don't we need one? We're clearly at war. When you can get shot in your own house like Botham Jean or Atatiana Jefferson, what else can you call it?

All deaths are tragic, but not all of them are surprising. When dudes are on the streets, running afoul of the law, the propensity for something happening is probably exacerbated. But when cops kill two people in their homes, what else can you call it but war?

You used to be able to tell yourself, "Well, he sold cigarettes," or "He wouldn't comply." But what do you say to these people who were just at home at night, and had white cops shoot them through a window or bust into their homes and kill them there? I mean, you're gonna run out of us to kill. You're killing "good ones" now.

FREEDOM, BUT NOT A FORK

There are people in America who think just not having slaves anymore was all we needed. Because you freed the slaves in 1865, we good. But it was a hundred years later before you gave us the ability to eat at the same restaurant as you. So you gave us freedom, but not a fork.

You gave us the right to not be slaves anymore, but then you changed the vagrancy laws, the housing laws, and the voting laws to make it almost impossible for us to *really* be free. All these changes were just designed to keep us slaves. You reincarnated the incarceration.

I WANT TO BE TREATED LIKE AMERICAN

I think America can do better for us. Let me tell you a story.

I travel a lot for work because I'm touring all the time. I probably spend $300,000 to $400,000 a year on airline tickets. I have maybe nine million air miles because I fly domestically every week. And because I fly American Airlines so much, I'm a ConciergeKey member. That's the top status; I don't even know how you get to be a ConciergeKey member—it's some kind of secret. There's nowhere I'm treated better. They meet me at the gate, come pick me up in a Cadillac—they're not fucking around.

I might be a god on American, but when I go other places, I'm just another black guy. Or worse, people think I work for my assistant, Derek.

Now granted, Derek looks like a model, so he's always going to get attention. I mean, I'm dope, but he looks like the Most Interesting Man in the World. So I'm used to it. But it's incredible how quickly you go from being king to just another nigger.

Recently, we were staying at the Ritz-Carlton in Orlando. Derek had my credit card and he was at the counter

checking us in. I remembered that I had to give him a letter, so I walked up to give it to Derek and this white man
goes, "HEY!"

Like that: *"HEY!"*

And he startled me. You know how your mouth goes
like a Cheerio when you're startled? Nigga, I have never
been so surprised. I just stopped short and my mouth
looked like a big O. I was *startled*.

He said, "What are you doing? The line's back here."
This guy's standing there with his wife and kids. And I
said, *"He* works for *me*. We were in line—and I just had
to get this letter." And I got mad that I was explaining
myself. I said, "By the way, I would never be that rude
where I would jump in front of somebody, a man with
his family." He said, "Well, I apologize." I said, "Not fast
enough."

Then Derek and I were waiting, having a drink while
they were bringing my bags up. The dude's wife walked by
on her way to the pool with her two little girls in their floats
and shit. She saw me and she mouthed, "I'm so sorry." You
know when a wife says something like that, she knows her
husband's an asshole.

But he was showing off for his family. "I'm gonna show
this nigger." And I'm like, "Man, do you see me?" White

people have a psychic confusion when they see a black man in the fucking Ritz.

But at American, it's different. Like I said, I'm an American god. So recently we were leaving L.A., and Derek and I were waiting to board. There's one lane for priority boarding, one for first class. ConciergeKey members board before first class, but when they called us this old white guy walked right past us—"Excuse me, excuse me"—to get on the plane. He just shoved past us. This guy had a flag lapel pin and a navy-blue blazer, khakis and tassel loafers—like straight from the country club. He was so dismissive. So he came barreling up to be at the front and tried to go ahead of us, but the flight attendant stuck her arm out like *BAM*. She full-on blocked him and said, "No, no, *they're* boarding first." She just did him like that: *BAM*. And I just started laughing looking at him. I was like, "*Wow.*" And then he said, "Well, I thought it was my turn. I thought I was first."

And that white man just could not believe it. This Asian American flight attendant made him wait while Derek and I boarded. He probably had never had that happen to him. And that's why he'll vote for Trump again: because a nigger, a beaner, and a fucking chink stopped him from taking his rightful place.

That was like a little bit of reparations right there. *I*

thought I was first. That's white America right there. American Airlines makes me feel how it feels to be a white man. That's probably the closest I get to being a white dude. So I don't blame him for being mad; I wouldn't want to give that shit up either.

I'm writing up this treaty because I want *America* to treat me like *American.*

WHY YOU HAVE TO SURRENDER

But D.L., why do I have to "surrender"? Shouldn't we be coming to some kind of a compromise?

You ever notice that whenever America makes "compromises," they're usually sacrificing black people? "Compromise" means "I'm giving up poor black people."

- **THE GREAT COMPROMISE**—gave rural states as many senators as populous states
- **THE THREE-FIFTHS COMPROMISE**—counted slaves as three-fifths of a person
- **THE MISSOURI COMPROMISE**—allowed Missouri to be a slave state
- **THE COMPROMISE OF 1850**—admitted a bunch of new slave states into the United States

Whenever there's a compromise, it's us doing the compromising. So . . . no more "compromises." We can come to an *understanding* or a *deal,* but we're not gonna compromise. *That's* why you have to surrender. Release yourselves from your racist delusions and address the real structural injustice that keeps black and brown people down. Remember, we got the numbers now.

WE'LL TRY TO IGNORE YOUR PROBLEMATIC HISTORY

If you're reluctant to sign this peace treaty, think of how we feel: we have to bargain with people who have shown themselves to be untrustworthy again and again. Let's start by acknowledging that white America's track record with upholding agreements is . . . not good. That shit has not ended well, ever since the first time a white guy offered a black guy a boat ride. *Man, I thought this was supposed to be a three-hour tour.*

No backsies, and no crossing your fingers behind your backs when you sign this thing. We'll be checking the fine print, because we know that's where you like to hide shit. And we'll be checking up to make sure you uphold your end of the bargain. Like your pal Reagan says: "Trust, but verify."

I don't want to start off too negative. I'm not trying to say that *all* white people can't be trusted. Of course, there are *good people on both sides.*

THIS ONE'S JUST LIKE THOSE OTHER TREATIES YOU SIGNED

If it's helpful, think of this treaty as something like the Indian treaties you all signed. What did the United States get from the Indians? Nothing except silence. They already took all their land. What was the goal, then? The goal was to make them not be a nuisance anymore. They were a pain in the ass. *What the fuck—you attack me with your dumb bows and arrows and now I have to kill all of you, and everybody thinks I'm an asshole.*

White people write treaties because they don't want to feel like assholes, basically. Treaties are an admission of something short of guilt. They're a way to buy peace and silence while saying, "Sorry, not sorry."

THE TERMS OF OUR PEACE TREATY

PRE-PREAMBLE

Treaties have to get written in official, fancy language: you know, "henceforth" and "having thus described" and so on. People write shit up that way to seem official, but also to be confusing. It's like the small print. That's just how treaties are. I'm not gonna try to trick you, white people, but I'm not about to get mine thrown out just because I wanted to keep it casual. So as we go along here, I'm going to put together a real *treaty* treaty, real official sounding.

And everybody knows that a treaty needs a preamble. I mean, shit: How're you gonna amble without a pre-amble?

PREAMBLE

A Peace Treaty Between White America and Black Folks

The search for peace between races must be guided by the following:

Black folks ("African Americans," "people of color," "those people") have decided, after four hundred years of oppression and discrimination, to come to the table and issue demands for a lasting peace with their oppressors. That's mighty big of them.

White people ("America"), having determined to hold a conference with the black folks, for the purpose of removing from their minds all causes of complaint, making them stop grousing, posting annoying memes to social media, and otherwise throwing shade, and establishing a firm and permanent friendship with them, recognize D.L. Hughley as sole agent for that purpose and affirm their intent to come to terms.

Recognizing that it is in the interest of all that racial harmony be established and racial animus shall no longer be the default;

Acknowledging that cooperation in this goal is of the essence and necessary, that peace may prosper, even if that means talking about things that upset the apple cart;

Acknowledging also that everyone's been a little hot under the collar for a while about all this stuff;

Convinced that the establishment of a firm foundation for the continuation and development of such cooperation on the basis of mutual understanding accords with the interests of harmony and peace;

Convinced also that a treaty ensuring this peace, by nature, must be specific and must cut the treacle;

Now, in order to accomplish the good design of this conference, the parties have agreed on the following articles, which, when ratified, shall be fully binding.

Damn, it's a pain to write like that.

WAIT, I DIDN'T AGREE TO ANYTHING!

*"But hold up, D.L.," you say. "I wasn't alive in 1846—
I wasn't even around in 1946—why the hell do I have
to pay you money for something that I didn't do?"*

I hear that. That's how a lot of white people feel. But
don't you see, it's not just about slavery. In this book I'm
going to explain how oppression keeps happening in the
most seemingly innocuous ways. I'm going to explain how
race is embedded in everything in American life today for
black people. So it's not just about slavery, and it's not all
about money.

If you want me to shut up, you have to at least hear me
out. If we're going to have peace, first you get a piece of my
mind.

WHITE PEOPLE SHALL CONSIDER REPARATIONS

R-R-R-REPARATIONS?!?

The word "reparations" is so scary to white people. They act like the idea of reparations is crazy. But support is growing, and now here we are at this treaty. Yes, so far, only 26 percent of Americans support some kind of compensation or payments to descendants of slaves. But most of them haven't read this book yet.

THE CASE FOR REPARATIONS

In 2014, Ta-Nehisi Coates made a powerful case for reparations in his essay titled, um, "The Case for Reparations." He chronicled the course of racial injustice in America and set the terms for the discussion of reparations since. Before that, everyone pretended like *Chappelle's Show* was the most serious representation of reparations: people buying liquor, cigarettes, and fried chicken. Coates argued not just for a bunch of checks being sent out, but for a reckoning with America's past:

> And so we must imagine a new country. Reparations—by which I mean the full acceptance of our collective biography and its consequences—is the price we must pay to see ourselves squarely. The recovering alcoholic may well have to live with his illness for the rest of his life. But at least he is not living a drunken lie. Reparations beckons us to reject the intoxication of hubris and see America as it is—the work of fallible humans.
>
> . . . What I'm talking about is more than recompense for past injustices—more than a handout, a payoff, hush money, or a reluctant bribe. What I'm talking

about is a national reckoning that would lead to spiritual renewal. Reparations would mean the end of scarfing hot dogs on the Fourth of July while denying the facts of our heritage. Reparations would mean the end of yelling "patriotism" while waving a Confederate flag. Reparations would mean a revolution of the American consciousness, a reconciling of our self-image as the great democratizer with the facts of our history.

If Coates's well-reasoned, eloquently presented, emotionally impactful essay didn't change your mind, what will? That shit is well said. But you all still didn't want to go for that. And the reason is, I don't think America wants to have "a national reckoning." I think what it wants is for us to shut the fuck up.

THAT'S SOME GOOD CHICKEN

I think that the closest we may have ever come to reparations was the Popeyes chicken sandwich.

Remember when reparations talk was hot and heavy? It was all over the news, the Democratic presidential candidates were all talking about it, there were hearings on Capitol Hill—and then all of a sudden, they come out with the Popeyes chicken sandwich.

It hooked our communities like the crack epidemic. Man, we were not prepared for it. Black people standing in line for an hour and a half for a chicken sandwich? How can anyone focus on reparations when all you can think about is whether you're gonna get your fix?

And this was no ordinary sandwich. It was diabolical. They must have studied our habits for years to get a sandwich that tapped into nigga-ness so succinctly. The *thought* that went into it! Sure, chicken; that's a basic element. That's a given. *Well, we got to give them soft bread. Black people love soft bread. And sauce with that.* But then to add the pickles? That's evil-genius-level shit. I mean, this sandwich is fucking irresistible. I don't know nobody who doesn't like this sandwich. It hit all black people like a plague: people with refined tastes and without. Rich and poor. People who love fast food and people who should know better. My daughter went to culinary school and she had to have it. And I know professors who cut class just for a taste. I heard they closed Foot Locker early. We were not prepared for it.

And we haven't heard anything about reparations since.

But you couldn't just let us have the sandwich, right? That'd be giving too much away. Then *you ran out of chicken*? How do you run out of chicken? Right now I have a dozen eggs in my refrigerator. That's twelve would-be chickens right there.

So it was purposeful. It was a conspiracy. You ran out of chicken just to keep us unsteady and on edge. The niggas wanted reparations, then they got their chicken sandwiches. And then the chicken ran out—so now it's all "When will the chicken come back?" instead of "Where's our money?"

And they won't even tell us when it's coming back. It's like your father. You know what I'm saying? They *say* it's because it was "experimental." That's two experiments I'll always hold against white society: the Tuskegee Syphilis Experiment and the Popeyes Chicken Experiment.

Well, I'm onto you. So that's the first article of this treaty: since the Constitution only counted us as three-fifths of a person—we should only have to pay three-fifths of the price of that sandwich.

Reparations Article 1a. Chicken Discount

It is thus decided that due to the Popeyes chicken sandwich being much beloved in the black community, but in suspiciously short supply, all such sandwiches shall be offered to black folks at a three-fifths discount.

THE MITCH McCONNELL PROBLEM

But before we got distracted, reparations was in the news. Four hundred years after the first slaves were brought to America, the Democrats in Congress held the first hearings on reparations in decades, taking up Representative John Conyers's H.R. 40 bill. First introduced thirty years before, this bill sought to establish a commission to study the institution of slavery and make recommendations for amends.

And in the 2020 presidential campaign, Democrats were at least discussing it. You could get fucked up in the primaries if you didn't have a reasonable answer to the issue. Candidates at least had to say, "Well, we have to put an exploratory committee together, do some research, etc." Nobody could just say, "Fuck it, it's unnecessary."

Predictably, there was pushback because a lot of white people thought they *already* gave reparations. Mitch McConnell, the Republican Senate majority leader, probably put it best:

> I don't think reparations for something that happened 150 years ago, for whom none of us currently living are responsible, is a good idea. We've tried to

deal with our original sin of slavery by fighting a civil war, by passing landmark civil rights legislation. We elected an African American president. . . . I don't think we should be trying to figure out how to compensate for it. First of all, it would be hard to figure out whom to compensate.

First of all: "*We* elected an African American president"? No, I guarantee *you* didn't. I guarantee you had nothing to do with it. *We* didn't do anything. For Mitch McConnell to put himself in a sentence like that is telling. McConnell spearheaded *opposition* to Obama. He's the one who said, "The single most important thing we want to achieve is for President Obama to be a one-term president." He blocked Obama's Supreme Court nominee Merrick Garland. So forget about McConnell taking responsibility for stuff that happened 150 years ago; how about taking responsibility for stuff that happened nine years ago?

White people want to claim credit for electing Obama, even if they voted against him. They want to take credit for civil rights legislation, after they opposed it. And they want to take credit for ending the Civil War, when all they did was lose it. We've moved forward *despite* their actions, not because of them. Everything black people got from

America, we got over the protests and anger and vitriol of white supremacy. Everything we can do, everything—playing baseball, going to dinner, using a bathroom—everything we've ever wanted to do, we had to do over the protests of old white men like McConnell.

And is it really that hard to figure out whom to compensate, Mitch? McConnell's lucky because NBC News did his homework for him. They found that both his paternal and maternal great-great-grandfathers, James McConnell and Richard Daley, owned slaves. According to county "Slave Schedules," they owned at least fourteen slaves in Alabama, all but two of them female. Four are classified as "mulatto." The only way you get a mulatto is for a black person and a white person to have sex, right? So that would mean that if his relatives owned those slaves, it's likely that they raped them. So right now, there's somebody sharing Mitch McConnell's name that is a relative of his. So "it would be hard to figure out whom to compensate"? Well, you could start at your next family reunion, actually. "Pass the potato salad and the reparations."

The sad part is that McConnell can say whether we have the conversation or not. He's the majority leader of the Senate. And I think it's weird that a dude whose great-great-grandparents owned slaves gets to decide whether we're gonna have a conversation about what they did. Shouldn't he recuse himself?

But whether you're in charge of the Senate or not, a lot of white folks feel like this. They weren't around, they didn't have anything to do with it. It isn't *their fault*. Well, it was *someone's* fault.

Sometimes history is important to white people and sometimes it isn't. They want to have their Confederate statues, right? But they weren't here for that. They want the patina of the war; they want to pay to remember it, just not pay to rectify it. They preserve battlefields, they re-create Civil War battles because they like the glory of it, just not how gory it was. They have selective amnesia. How did white people get to be who they are today? On whose backs? They want to remember when it suits their purposes and not remember when it doesn't.

WHAT KIND OF REPARATIONS?

But like I say: We're not gonna shut up about it. This unpleasant state of affairs will continue if you just want to put your fingers in your ears. If you want everything to stay the same, with all the conflict and bad feelings, what can I say? But if you want change, try to engage in at least the thought experiment of what reparations might look like.

It's incredible what white people can accomplish when they want something. *I believe in you!*

So are we talking about cash payments? Is everybody affected by slavery getting a check? Maybe. But there are other ways to pay reparations too. You don't have to give money, but you could give low-interest loans. You could cut the tax rate. You could make sure everybody receives an equal education. You could make sure everybody gets fairly financed for a house. It's at least worth talking about, right?

And it's not like nobody's ever tried to figure out reparations. Republicans act like it's just too complicated. But look around: somehow you worked out how to pay other people before.

REPARATIONS ALREADY HAPPENED, SORT OF

Mitch McConnell is right about one thing: in fact, historically, payments for slavery have already been paid. Unfortunately, those reparations were paid the other way: they were paid to former *owners* of slaves.

For example, in 1825 France forced the government of Haiti to pay reparations to former slave owners after Haiti's slaves revolted against their colonial rulers and founded an independent government. Under threat of being invaded,

Haiti had to pay 150 million francs for the loss of French "property." Haiti had to take loans and pay this ransom with interest for 124 years, from 1825 to 1947. It's pretty easy to become a "shithole" country when a rich country has a gun to your head.

And you know, when your property gets took, you file an insurance claim. It was routine practice to have insurance on "cargo," in this case, slaves. So if you throw your slaves overboard, who's to know that your insurance claim isn't right? How many millions of black people were killed in the Middle Passage between Africa and the New World is unknown, but one documented incident was the Zong Massacre in 1781. After an outbreak of illness, the ship's captain decided to murder 132 enslaved people by throwing them overboard. Fifty-four people were chained together and then drowned, and over the next few days, another seventy-eight were thrown overboard. We know about it because the owners filed an insurance claim for the "loss."

And when slavery was banned in England in 1833, the British government paid three thousand families that had owned slaves for the loss of their property. So reparations for slavery isn't such a crazy idea, it's just that white folks tend to get the check.

WHERE'S MY FORTY ACRES AND A MULE?

So fine, weren't we all promised "forty acres and a mule"? Spike Lee didn't just make that shit up, right? Everyone's heard of that, but what the hell was it?

At the tail end of the Civil War, General William Tecumseh Sherman issued Special Field Order No. 15, which called for giving four hundred thousand acres of coastline to freed slaves in forty-acre increments. A little later, he added the mule part.

Sherman wasn't just being a nice guy; he was trying to stick it to the white rice farmers of the South and solve a problem at the same time. The problem was what to do with all the freed peoples of the South who had no resources of their own. Sherman consulted with a group of black preachers from Savannah, Georgia, to come up with solutions. The leader of the group, Garrison Frazier, a Baptist minister and himself a former slave, argued for land: "The way we can best take care of ourselves is to have land, and turn it and till it by our own labor." Giving everyone forty acres was a way to keep ex-slaves self-sufficient and allow Sherman to keep marching northward. People were actually given land from this order. By June 1865, approximately forty thousand freedmen had settled four hundred thousand acres.

But you know there's no way they're gonna give niggas beachfront property. I think Lincoln got killed by Century 21. Somebody check and see if John Wilkes Booth was wearing a gold blazer. After Lincoln's assassination, President Andrew Johnson came in and he was like, "No. Fuck that," and he made everyone give everything back.

It must have been awkward. Stepping up to some old white guy's plantation, ringing the bell: Ding-dong. *Hey, man, thanks for letting me borrow your mule.*

And that was the end of that first bit of reparations. So let's start there. I mean, I don't know if it makes sense for all the black folks to get forty acres and a mule anymore, but *it's something*.

Let's see: If all the black folk in America each get 40 acres, that's 40 × 42 million people. That's 1.68 billion acres, and America only has like 2.43 billion. That would be most of the lower forty-eight states. And black people are not gonna live in Alaska, so we already got a problem. If you give us all the land you owe us, where the fuck are you all gonna live? The last thing we need is to deal with a bunch of angry white folks renting property from us, not paying rent on time, making a mess and being shitty tenants. Without that pride of homeownership, you just can't trust white folks to not trash the place and leave us holding the bill.

Plus, with global warming, half this land's gonna be underwater in a few years. And you know black folks don't like to swim. No, I think it's too late to hand out all that land.

And without the land, what's the point of handing out forty-two million mules? First of all, mules are actually a cross between a donkey and a horse. Without getting into a whole biology lesson—do you know how a mule is made? *Sometimes when a horse and a donkey love each other very much* . . . So how the hell are you going to find enough horses and donkeys to make that many mules? I'd think it'd take a special horse to love a donkey that much. And forty-two million of them—I don't see it.

So fine; you don't have the land and you don't have the mules. So you reneged on that and it's time to renegotiate. We need a new deal. A New New Deal.

RADISH MONEY

After President Johnson canceled the order providing land for ex-slaves, many of them were relegated to poverty and forced into sharecropping for their former masters and landowners. Thousands of people were removed from land they had been given under Sherman's Special Field Order No. 15.

But it wasn't like reparations talks were *over*. It was still discussed. On one side were the former slave owners who wanted to be compensated for their lost "property," never mind that they just lost a war over it. And on the other side were the formerly enslaved, whose labor had enriched America over the previous several hundred years.

Groups of former slaves pushed for reparations in the form of pensions in the 1890s and early 1900s. The main group spearheading this was the National Ex-Slave Mutual Relief, Bounty and Pension Association, the MRB&PA, led by Callie House. Callie House was a widow, a former slave, a mother of five, and a badass. Her plan called for pensions based on an ex-slave's age: people seventy and older would get $500 and $15 per month for life; those in their sixties would get $300 and $12 per month; those in their fifties would get $100 and $8 a month, and anyone under fifty would get $4 per month. Not much, but you know in 1899 you could buy yourself a delicious plate of radishes for fifteen cents or some green apple fritters in rum sauce for sixty cents, whatever those were.

The plan was similar to Civil War pensions for disabled soldiers, so it should have seemed reasonable. Y'all could have gotten off cheap back then. But instead, the government infiltrated and undermined the MRB&PA, accusing its officers of fraud. Hmm, the government investigating a black organization and seeking to undermine it? Where have I heard this before? The Bureau of Pensions, the Post Office Department, and the Justice Department all actively worked against the movement, especially after Callie House brought a class-action lawsuit against the U.S. Treasury in 1915 asking for $68 million, the amount of tax revenue earned from slave labor on cotton from 1862 to 1868.

The lawsuit failed, and eventually the Post Office Department charged House with mail fraud. I like my post office delivering mail, not indictments. After an all-white-male jury convicted her, she spent a year in jail. Even though it was a frame-up, the slave pension movement fell apart after.

LOOK AT THE GERMANS

So America has fucked up on reparations a few times, but we can look around and see how other countries have used reparations to apologize and atone for their behavior. For instance, West Germany paid money to Israel after World War II. At the time, the first Israeli prime minister, David Ben-Gurion, argued for reparations "so that the murderers do not become the heirs as well."

But many Israelis didn't want to take money from Germans, because they felt like they'd be taking blood money. And many Germans felt like they hadn't done anything. According to *The Jewish Press,* "only 34 percent of the German public believed that Germany owed Jews anything at all, and 21 percent still believed that *the Jews themselves were responsible for what had happened to them during the Holocaust*" (emphasis in original).

But the agreement ended up passing, and today more than $70 billion has been paid in reparations. These weren't warm and fuzzy negotiations, there wasn't total agreement, but still they got paid. And in 2000, German companies that had used slave labor in the war created a foundation to compensate people. It's not like this has made up for the Holocaust or made many Jews want to spend their vacations in Baden-Baden, but it's *something.*

If former Nazis and Jews can sit down and hammer out a settlement, why can't white America and black people?

SOME PEOPLE GOT PAID
JAPANESE GOT PAID

It's not like the American government hasn't ever paid anyone money or apologized to *anyone.* In 1988, President Reagan signed the Civil Liberties Act, compensating people of Japanese descent who were imprisoned in camps during World War II. During the war, 120,000 people were put in internment camps because of racist fears after the Pearl Harbor attack. After years of pressure from people whose property and livelihood had been taken away, the government issued a formal apology and $20,000 to compensate each surviving victim.

AND ITALIANS . . .

Oh, and did I mention that Italians were given reparations? I'll tell you about that one later, but damn—Italians? Japanese, Italians, Jews—I mean, we gotta be in line before the Irish, right?

AND OTHERS

Some white people get hung up, or like to pretend to get hung up, on the mystery of who might have been enslaved by whom. How can we know who benefited from slavery? How can we know who was enslaved? How can we possibly figure it out? It's too hard, so why try?

Except this didn't all happen thousands of years ago! We're not trying to figure out if King Tut liked sausages for breakfast or if Julius Caesar had a horse named Betsy. This isn't ancient history. Slavery ended just 150 years ago.

And just because the government is sitting on its hands, that doesn't mean that nothing can be done. Some people have tried to do the right thing, after they did the wrong thing. At Georgetown University, students voted to increase their tuition to pay reparations to descendants of 272 slaves who had been owned by the school. In 1838, the Jesuits who ran Georgetown sold their slaves to raise money. This sale stands out because of the large number of slaves sold and the fact that it was *Catholic priests* doing the selling. That's fucked up, but maybe not even in the top ten most fucked-up things Catholic priests have done.

After student protests and a financial push from alumni, these 272 people were researched and their history traced, and genealogists were able to find almost four thousand descendants of the slaves sold in 1838. It's not some abstract, unknowable history. It's not always easy, because paper trails are scarce, but with some effort it can be done.

So now, along with the students' vote to increase tuition, Georgetown has issued an apology, renamed several buildings, and provided admissions preference to descendants. Is that enough? Who knows? But it's a start, and an acknowledgment of wrongdoing.

While we're renaming buildings, I want to make sure that we're not picking all the obvious people. Sure, we could name another building for Sojourner Truth, and she deserves every building she gets. But I think we should name some buildings or scholarships after people who never really got to reach their full potential because of slavery and the oppression of racism. Not the people who triumphed and overcame racism. It's easy to name buildings after people who were triumphant.

Nipsey Hussle should have a building, for example. It should be all cats like him. The ones who, if not for systemic oppression, might have been something. They would never have gotten accepted into genteel society, but I'm sure their shit gets played at homecoming games.

Reparations Article 1b. Nipsey Hall

In recognition of the fact that buildings are named after old white guys, some of whom were involved in the very systemic racism and oppression that have brought us to this fraught moment of racial tension, we hereby establish a new naming criterion for buildings in universities, cities, and other public institutions. Consideration shall be given to badass, dope niggas whose time passed too soon and who might not previously have been accepted as people to bear in tribute.

With students and activists pushing them, a bunch of different colleges, including Harvard, Brown, Columbia, and the University of Virginia have put together commissions and issued apologies for their ties to the slave trade. And some religious institutions, like churches and convents, have done work to figure out their slave-owning past and make amends.

The Virginia Theological Seminary just set up a $1.7 million reparations fund. And the Catholic sisters of the Society of the Sacred Heart created a fund to finance scholarships for descendants of the 150 slaves the society once owned in Louisiana and Missouri. This is moral leadership from institutions that preach morality. But it wouldn't have happened if the people in charge just threw up their hands or shrugged off the responsibility of the past.

These institutions are facing up to history. Why won't you?

I think a big problem is that white people and black people have totally different perceptions of America. Everyone feels emotional about the whole thing, and yet in so many ways our interests align. Try not to think of this as a lose-lose. What if I could get you to see it our way? Would that take away the sting of surrender?

ARTICLE II

HISTORY BOOKS SHALL BE ALIGNED

OUR HISTORY BOOKS AND YOURS

Suffice it to say, black people's history books and white people's textbooks wouldn't match up. But let's try to get on the same page. A lot of people don't really know the history of how we got here, or they got bad facts. It shouldn't be surprising that some of the same people who enslaved us or justified oppressing us also wrote the history books.

So let's look at the history of slavery and oppression in America. How can we judge what we owe each other if we aren't operating from the same facts? Let's see if you can put yourself in our shoes, see if you think you'd still be pissed if this were your history.

IN THE BEGINNING . . .

The deal for black people in America changed almost overnight.

In 1619, the first enslaved Africans were brought to Virginia, where they were sold to colonists of Jamestown. These were people seized from a Portuguese slave ship by an English ship, then sold to colonists in exchange for food.

Initially, slavery was a bit *informal;* everyone, black or white, was considered an indentured servant. It was something of a handshake deal, or maybe a *handcuff* deal. Maybe it wasn't a lot different from slavery. If you were a black indentured servant in 1619 Virginia, I bet you *felt* like a slave. Probably nobody said, "Hey, man, don't feel so bad—you're only an indentured servant!" *Feels pretty slave-y.* That said, some of the first slaves brought to America were able to buy their freedom or have kids who weren't slaves.

But after a little while, the deal got switched up on black folks. It must have been pretty fucked up to be a black man in colonial Virginia when these new laws were getting passed, taking away freedom after freedom. Look at this list from Historic Jamestowne's website:

- **1630s:** "Customary practice to hold some Negroes in a form of life service." *Some. Okay, all right. At least it's not like every Negro is a slave . . .*
- **1639:** "All persons except Negroes are to be with Arms and Ammunition." *It does make me nervous that us black folk can't have guns, but they said, "Look, we got you—you don't need to hold on to a piece."*
- **1640:** "John Punch, a runaway indentured Servant, first documented slave for life." *John Punch got slapped, I guess.*
- **1662:** "Slavery was recognized in the statutory law of the colony." *Oh, okay, now it's a little less informal.*
- **1667:** "Baptism does not bring freedom." Baptized Africans are no longer exempt from slavery. *White people think they're bigger than God. What would Jesus do?*
- **1680:** "Blacks could not congregate in large numbers." *Huh, why are there only four other brothers at this party?*
- **1692:** "Negroes must give up ownership of horses, cattle or hogs." *How am I gonna ride the fuck out of here without my horse . . . Oh, I see . . .*

So the picture we have of black people being brought over as slaves is one that didn't have to be. It was a devolution of rights, taken away in pieces. By 1705, the Virginia Slave Codes were passed, and slavery was codified in America. In only a few decades, slavery became a thing America relied on, and the subjugation of black people began.

LIFE, LIBERTY, AND THE PURSUIT OF HAPPINESS

So from the very beginning of America, we were being cut out of the deal. It's interesting that when Thomas Jefferson was writing the Declaration of Independence in 1776, he had slaves. He wrote the words:

> We hold these Truths to be self-evident, that all men are created equal, that they are endowed by their Creator with certain unalienable Rights, that among these are Life, Liberty and the pursuit of Happiness.

"All men" seems straightforward enough, but what's this asterisk here? I don't even know where they put the fine print on a scroll, but if you find it, it says, *All men are created equal . . . except you niggers. Get me some tea!* Right?

Apparently, Jefferson's first draft did have some shit about slaves in it. One of the things he accused King George of was:

> He has waged cruel war against human nature itself, violating it's [*sic*] most sacred rights of life & liberty in the persons of a distant people who never offended

him, captivating & carrying them into slavery in another hemisphere, or to incur miserable death in their transportation thither.

So he blamed King George for slavery, called it a "cruel war against human nature itself," all while owning slaves. Jefferson was . . . a complicated guy. But we knew that from his "relationship" with his slave Sally Hemings. So the other part about slaves that didn't make it into the final draft was about the king inciting slaves to rise up against the colonies:

He is now exciting those very people to rise in arms among us, and to purchase that liberty of which he has deprived them, & murdering the people upon whom he also obtruded them: thus paying off former crimes committed against the liberties of one people, with crimes which he urges them to commit against the lives of another.

Yeah, that's complicated: slave owner hates on slavery, but doesn't want slaves to be freed because they might murder their owners. White people worried about black people rising up for freedom? Sounds familiar.

But none of that made it into the final draft anyway;

Jefferson had to keep the Southern delegates happy to get the thing signed, so everyone agreed to scrap that part. They had to come to a *compromise*. Once again, some old white guys from the South cut us out of the deal.

THREE-FIFTHS OF A MAN

And when the Founding Fathers got together to write up the Constitution, things didn't get any better for black people. See, what happens when you get a bunch of white guys in a room is you get things like the Three-Fifths Compromise. When the Founders were trying to come up with the legislative branch, they had to figure out how to account for everyone. Some people argued for not counting slaves at all; others wanted them counted. So everyone met in the middle to count each slave as three-fifths of a person. I bet a lot of us have felt like three-fifths of a person after a late night out, but that shit usually lifts around noon.

This worked well enough for everyone—well, the *white* everyones—along with a couple of extra promises that importing slaves was okay for another twenty years and that fugitive slaves would be returned to their owners. Ultimately, it would take the Civil War to undo the slave trade in America, but we're still stuck with the compromised form of representation that gives every state two senators, regardless of how many people live there. So Wyoming gets two senators and California gets two senators. This continues to skew power to the South centuries later. More Americans live in Los Angeles than live in Mississippi, but Mississippians get to elect a redneck like Senator Cindy Hyde-Smith, who made jokes about public hangings and went to a segregation academy. Meanwhile, I don't get to vote for an extra Senator Magic Johnson.

SLAVERY WAS BAD

I shouldn't need to say this, but let's all get on the same page about something: slavery was bad.

I do need to say it, however, because even though I never see any white people *signing up to be slaves,* I still hear people trying to make it seem like slavery wasn't, you know, *bad.* Some of these people aren't saying it was *good* so much as they're saying it wasn't *that bad. Look on the bright side, black people!*

Take the criticism of the movie *12 Years a Slave,* which conservatives seemed to think was going to be about twelve great years. James Bowman, film critic for *American Spectator,* complained about director Steve McQueen's choices: "If ever in slavery's 250-year history in North America there were a kind master or a contented slave, as in the nature of things there must have been, here and there, we may be sure that Mr. McQueen does not want us to hear about it." *Why wasn't there a nice slave owner in the movie about abducting someone and forcing him into slavery?*

And sure, it's shameful that slaves helped to build the White House, but it wasn't all that bad according to Bill O'Reilly: "Slaves that worked there were well fed and had decent lodgings provided by the government." *It wasn't so bad: they got a lunch break and a shack to live in!*

The cool thing is that we don't have to rely on conservatives to tell us what it was like to be a slave. We can read for ourselves. In the 1930s, writers working for the Works Progress Administration interviewed many of the still-living former slaves and recorded their stories.

I know when I'm reading about slaves, I use Morgan Freeman's voice. I don't know what you all use, but feel free to fill in Samuel L. Jackson, Viola Davis, or Whoopi Goldberg as necessary.

Does this sound "bad" or "not so bad":

One day I remembers my brother, January, was caught over seein a gal on de next plantation. He had a pass, but de time on it done gib out. Well sir, when Massa found out dat he was a hour late, he got as mad as a hive of bees. So when January he come home, de massa took down his long mule skinner and tied him a rope to a pine tree. He strip his shirt off and said: "Now, nigger, I'm goin to teach you some sense."

Wid dat he started layin on de lashes. January was a big, fine lookin nigger, finest I ever seed. He was just four years older dan me, an when de mass begin a beatin him, January never said a word. De massa got madder and madder cause he couldn't make January holla.

"What's de matter wid you, nigger?" he say. "Don't it hurt?"

January, he never said nothin, and de massa keep a beatin till little streams of blood started flowin down January's chest, but he never holler. His lips was a quiverin' and his body was a shakin, but his mouth it never open; and all de while I sat on my mammy's and pappy's steps a-cryin.

—*William Colbert, 93, Alabama*

Bad or not so bad:

Aunt Cheyney was jus' out of bed with a sucklin' baby one time, and she run away. Some say that was nother baby of massa's breedin'. She don't come to the house to nurse her baby, so they misses her and old Solomon gits the nigger hounds and takes her trail. They gits near her and she grabs a limb and tries to hoist herself in a tree, but them dogs grab her and pull her down. The men hollers them onto her, and the dogs tore her naked and ate the breasts plumb off her body. She got well and lived to be a old woman, but nother woman has to suck her baby and she ain't got no sign of breasts no more.

—*Mary Reynolds, 105, Texas*

Bad or not so bad:

My grandmother, and my mother were both freed like this, but what they called "nigger traders" captured them and two or three others, and they took them just like they would animals, and sold them, that was how "Ples" Holbert got my mother. My grandmother was sent to Texas. My mother said she wrote and had one letter from my grandmother after that, but she never saw her again.

—*Clayton Holbert, 86, Kansas*

Bad, right? So let's just put this to rest: slavery was bad.

WAS SLAVERY THE CAUSE OF THE CIVIL WAR?

D.L., was slavery the cause of the Civil War?

Yep. But don't take my word for it. Take the word of Alexander Stephens, the Confederacy's vice president:

> Our new government is founded upon exactly the opposite idea; its foundations are laid, its cornerstone rests, upon the great truth that the negro is not equal to the white man; that slavery subordination to the superior race is his natural and normal condition. This, our new government, is the first, in the history of the world, based upon this great physical, philosophical, and moral truth.

Wasn't it about states' rights or something?

Yeah, the states' rights to have slaves! Here's what the states said when they declared their secession from the Union:

> **MISSISSIPPI:** "Our position is thoroughly identified with the institution of slavery—the greatest material interest of the world."

SOUTH CAROLINA: "A geographical line has been drawn across the Union, and all the States north of that line have united in the election of a man to the high office of President of the United States, whose opinions and purposes are hostile to slavery. He is to be entrusted with the administration of the common Government, because he has declared that that 'Government cannot endure permanently half slave, half free,' and that the public mind must rest in the belief that slavery is in the course of ultimate extinction."

TEXAS: "In all the non-slave-holding States, in violation of that good faith and comity which should exist between entirely distinct nations, the people have formed themselves into a great sectional party, now strong enough in numbers to control the affairs of each of those States, based upon an unnatural feeling of hostility to these Southern States and their beneficent and patriarchal system of African slavery, proclaiming the debasing doctrine of equality of all men, irrespective of race or color—a doctrine at war with nature, in opposition to the experience of mankind, and in violation of the plainest revelations of Divine Law."

To pretend that the Civil War was about states' rights beyond the "right to have slaves" is nonsense. A lot of this bullshit was originally a way to make Southern people feel better about themselves after they got their asses kicked defending chaining people up, forcing them to work, raping them, and tearing apart their families. Yeah, that can *feel bad*.

That's why so many people still cling to the "Lost Cause" ideology that tried to reframe the secession of the South as a struggle to maintain a Southern way of life, to maintain states' rights, and *definitely, definitely* not just about slavery. Even though the leaders of the Southern states said it was about slavery, Lost Cause proponents pretended it was about a noble conflict, instead of a white supremacist economic model.

White people don't want the blame for slavery. And you don't get credit for ending it either. On the Fox News show *Outnumbered*, conservative commentator Katie Pavlich said, "They keep blaming America for the sin of slavery. But the truth is, throughout human history, slavery has existed, and America came along as the first country to end it within 150 years. And we get no credit for that, to move forward and try and make good on that."

Only 150 years? That's slower than Interstate 405 on a Friday.

And Newt Gingrich wants to get credit for the "several hundred thousand white Americans who died in the Civil War in order to free the slaves." See, I thought Newt represented Georgia. Isn't Georgia in the South?

Or take Ben Shapiro: "There was a national apology for slavery. It was called the Civil War where 700,000 Americans died." Um, Ben—that's a *total*. It didn't seem like half of those people were apologizing. Next time send flowers.

RECONSTRUCTION: A NEW HOPE

I'm not going to relitigate the whole Civil War. But you know the end of the story: we got our "freedom."

With the end of the Civil War, America had to figure out how to put all its pieces back together. Reconstruction, the period right after the war, from about 1865 to 1877, was a time when our basic rights got established, as did a lot of the lies still told about us. Embittered Southerners tried to reassert white supremacy after their loss. A racist, horrible president tried to let them do it. And finally, white people just got tired of the whole thing and let black folks down. It's the same kind of shit we're trying to prevent with this treaty!

After Lincoln's assassination, it was up to President Andrew Johnson to oversee Reconstruction. He wanted to let the Southern states dictate their own terms, even though they lost the war. Maybe it had something to do with the fact that he was, um, an unlikely champion for ex-slaves. "This is a country for white men, and by God, as long as I am President, it shall be a government for white men," he wrote in 1866. *Okay.*

So-called Radical Republicans opposed Johnson and pushed for stricter terms for readmitting former Southern states back into the Union and for ensuring ex-slaves had rights in the postwar era. You have to remember that back then Republicans were basically Democrats and Democrats were basically Republicans. That's why Republicans nowadays are always trying to claim that they are "the party of Lincoln" when they pretend to care about black people. If you gotta go back to the motherfucker on the penny, you've gotta update your résumé.

Right after the war ended, the Southern states had passed "black codes" that gave black people some rights, but didn't allow them to vote, work freely, serve on juries, or testify against white people in court. Using "vagrancy" laws, local governments could round up black people they felt weren't employed enough and force them into involuntary labor. *You're not a slave; you're an ex-slave doing involuntary labor.*

But the Radical Republicans pushed back, passing the Civil Rights Act of 1866, overriding Johnson's veto. The Thirteenth Amendment, banning slavery, had passed a year earlier. They then passed the Reconstruction Acts, again over Johnson's veto, setting harder terms for the states to reenter the Union. These included creating new state constitutions, which had to be approved by Congress. They passed the Fourteenth and Fifteenth Amendments, ensuring legal equality and giving the vote to black men.

Over the next few years, a newly empowered black political class emerged. Blacks voted in large numbers and elected interracial governments that had never been seen before. The number of black people in government went from zero to about two thousand—everyone from sheriffs to senators. It wasn't exactly Wakanda, but it was still pretty incredible.

This new political power led to big achievements like in South Carolina, where a biracial legislature came together to write a new state constitution and pass reforms like creating the first public school system of the South. It's crazy to think about now: several years before, blacks were enslaved, and now they were sitting at the table as equals in government.

It didn't last long. Violence and terrorism by the Ku Klux Klan and other groups spread and suppressed blacks.

In 1868, about a thousand black people were killed in racial violence. And in the 1868 U.S. presidential election, Republicans lost Georgia to Democrats because voter intimidation prevented black turnout. In Colfax, Louisiana, in 1873, 150 black people were killed by white supremacists to overturn an election.

By the time of the 1876 presidential election, the handwriting was on the wall. After years of war, then several cycles of white supremacist violence, the Northern Republican advocates for Reconstruction were fed up. Then there was a contested election where nobody got a majority of electoral votes. It was crazy—a constitutional crisis ensued, and a deal was struck. You know, a *compromise*. The Compromise of 1876. This put the Republican Rutherford B. Hayes in the White House but forced the withdrawal of all federal troops from the South, ceding effective control back to the white supremacists.

It's these white supremacists, the same motherfuckers who lost the Civil War and created the Klan and the Jim Crow laws of the South, who wrote the history books. They portrayed Reconstruction as a failure of black self-rule, instead of the violent oppression of a black minority. They rewrote history with their "Lost Cause" as the winner.

THE TOTALLY DUMB, WACKY LAWS OF JIM CROW

The era of "Jim Crow" laws had begun. Roughly speaking, these were laws and rules asserting racial segregation and white supremacy. They imposed restrictions on voting, transportation, marriage, and every other facet of life in America for black people, all the way through until the civil rights movement. You already know that people had to ride on different parts of the bus, use different water fountains, and so forth. But white supremacy is so virulent that laws were made about shit you'd think wouldn't even be worth fucking with:

MENTAL HOSPITALS (GEORGIA): "The Board of Control shall see that proper and distinct apartments are arranged for said patients, so that in no case shall Negroes and white persons be together." *If you had a crazy black dude who thought he was Napoleon, which ward did you put him in?*

BARBERS (GEORGIA): "No colored barber shall serve as a barber [to] white women or girls." *Barbershops remain segregated to this day, but you know, it's okay by me.*

CIRCUS TICKETS (LOUISIANA): "All circuses, shows, and tent exhibitions, to which the attendance of . . . more than one race is invited or expected to attend shall provide for the convenience of its patrons not less than two ticket offices with individual ticket sellers, and not less than two entrances to the said performance, with individual ticket takers and receivers." *They keep the lions and the elephants in the same tent, but the blacks and the whites in different ones?*

THE BLIND (LOUISIANA): "The board of trustees shall . . . maintain a separate building . . . on separate ground for the admission, care, instruction, and support of all blind persons of the colored or black race." *If there's anywhere that color shouldn't matter, it's in a house for blind people, right?*

GAMES (ALABAMA): "It shall be unlawful for a negro and white person to play together or in company with each other in any game of cards or dice, dominoes or checkers." *Damn, it's fucked up that you couldn't play a game of Boggle together.*

WELL-KNOWN UNKNOWNS

But nobody was in much of a Boggle mood anyway.

The history of racial violence in America is so crazy that white people don't believe it when they see it. The first episode of HBO's *The Watchmen* started with the Tulsa Race Massacre, but a lot of people thought that it was made up. They didn't know that it was depicting a real event where hundreds of black people were killed and thirty-five city blocks of Tulsa, including "Black Wall Street," were destroyed by white vigilantes. Why isn't this in the history books? Why don't more people know about it? It only happened in 1921—but it was buried and whitewashed. Not a single person was punished. So they won't give us justice, but they'll give us a TV show.

Donald Rumsfeld once said, "There are known knowns; there are things we know we know. We also know there are known unknowns; that is to say we know there are some things we do not know. But there are also unknown unknowns—the ones we don't know we don't know."

I'll add a category: there are well-known unknowns. There's shit that's unknown to all you white folks but is well-known to us. And because of that, you need a little education before you can judge whether your understanding of race in America is well informed. A lot of times you don't know it because it's so horrible, no one would admit that it happened. It's so horrible, you go, "That's bad—it can't be right." It is right. All of this shit happened in *America:*

1811: NEW ORLEANS SLAVE REVOLT

A group of slaves rallied an army of almost five hundred slaves to take over plantations north of New Orleans and then march to conquer the city. They battled the U.S. military and a white planter militia but were overwhelmed. In the brutal aftermath, militia members chopped off the leader's hands and burned him. They then executed and beheaded more than one hundred slaves, put their heads on spikes, and lined them along the river so when people came by, they would see the heads. "Their Heads, which decorate our Levee, all the way up the coast . . . look like crows sitting on long poles," wrote one traveler.

It was such a well-organized rebellion that it was basically erased from the history books.

1831: NAT TURNER'S REBELLION

Nat Turner led a slave revolt in Virginia, gathering almost one hundred slaves in an uprising that killed fifty-one white people. He was able to stay at large for almost two months before getting captured and killed. Throughout his rebellion, the rebels killed white people, but spared a few homes because Turner believed the poor white inhabitants "thought no better of themselves than they did of negroes." Southerners lived in terror that another Nat Turner might rise up and kill them in a similar organized attack.

1887: THIBODAUX MASSACRE OF SUGARCANE WORKERS

A group of striking black sugarcane workers was attacked in Thibodaux, Louisiana, after white vigilantes were brought in to break the strike. Gunmen ordered black men out of their houses and shot them. The posses killed sixty black Americans and yet no one was prosecuted or brought to justice.

1893: THE PUBLIC TORTURE OF HENRY SMITH

Lynchings weren't necessarily spontaneous outbreaks of violence. In 1893, a seventeen-year-old black man was captured by a mob after having been accused of raping and murdering a white child. He was brought by train back to Paris, Texas, where the townspeople had assembled a platform in the middle of town. He was then tortured and burned alive in front of ten thousand people. The *Fort Worth Gazette* reported the horrifying details:

A tinner's furnace was brought on with IRONS HEATED WHITE.

Taking one, Vance thrust it under first one and then the other side of his victim's feet, who, helpless, writhed as the flesh SCARRED AND PEELED from the bones.

Slowly, inch by inch, up his legs the iron was drawn and redrawn, only the nervous jerky twist of the muscles showing the agony being induced. When his body was reached and the iron was pressed to the most tender part of his body he broke silence for the first time and a prolonged SCREAM OF AGONY rent the air.

Slowly, across and around the body, slowly upward traced the irons. The withered scarred flesh marked the progress of the awful punishment. By turns Smith screamed, prayed, begged and cursed his tormentors. When his face was reached HIS TONGUE WAS SILENCED by fire and thenceforth he only moaned or gave a cry that echoed over the prairie like the wail of a wild animal.

Then his EYES WERE PUT OUT, not a fingerbreadth of his body being unscathed. His executioners gave way. They were Vance, his brother-in-law, and

Vance's son, a boy of 15 years of age. When they gave over punishing Smith they left the platform.

This was all done with the approval of law enforcement, the media, and the public.

1917: THE EAST ST. LOUIS "RACE RIOT"

After a car of white occupants drove through the black neighborhood of East St. Louis, Illinois, randomly shooting at people, two white policemen were mistakenly killed by residents who thought they were the shooters. In retaliation for this and amid labor tensions, a group of white rioters killed one hundred black people and destroyed over $400,000 in property. A reporter from the *St. Louis Post-Dispatch* described the indiscriminate killings:

I saw man after man, with hands raised, pleading for his life, surrounded by groups of men—men who had never seen him before and knew nothing about him except that he was black—and saw them administer the historic sentence of intolerance, death by stoning. I saw one of these men, almost dead from a savage shower of stones, hanged with a clothesline.

1919: THE RED SUMMER

During a year of widespread white mob attacks in more than three dozen cities, hundreds of black people were killed. Black soldiers returning from duty in World War I were especially targeted and fought back. A partial list of the violence:

- **JENKINS COUNTY, GEORGIA:** A mob burned a church down, lynched several people, and destroyed three black Masonic lodges.
- **CHARLESTON, SOUTH CAROLINA:** White U.S. Navy sailors led a riot that killed six black men and injured many more.
- **LONGVIEW, TEXAS:** Whites attacked the black area of town, killing people and burning property before the National Guard took control.
- **WASHINGTON, D.C.:** White soldiers rioted and beat black people on the street; the National Guard was called in after four days and fifteen deaths.
- **CHICAGO, ILLINOIS:** A black teenager was stoned for being on the wrong side of a segregated beach, sparking violence. There were at least 38 fatalities, 537 injuries, and 1,000 black families left homeless.

- **OMAHA, NEBRASKA:** A crowd of ten thousand white rioters surrounded and burned down a courthouse to lynch a black prisoner. They hanged him and burned his body, then attacked black businesses and homes before troops restored order.
- **ELAINE, ARKANSAS:** White planters organized a militia against black sharecroppers who sought to unionize. Over several days, they killed between 100 and 237 black people.

1921: TULSA RACE MASSACRE

A white mob attempted to lynch a black teen being held on bogus charges. They gathered around the courthouse and tried to force their way in. A group of armed black men arrived to defend him but was outnumbered by a huge crowd of whites. After a battle, black residents retreated to the Greenwood District, the black neighborhood of Tulsa containing "Black Wall Street." Thousands of white residents then attacked Greenwood, shooting unarmed black residents and burning homes and businesses. All of this was done in plain view of law enforcement and with the participation of whites who had been "deputized." When the National Guard arrived, they imprisoned the black Tulsans and kept them at a local fairground. Between one hundred and three hundred people were killed and more than eight thousand people were made homeless.

1943: DETROIT RACE RIOT

In 1942, white resistance to allowing black families to move into the Sojourner Truth Housing Project sparked racial tension. A year later, fighting, riots, and attacks escalated after false rumors of an assault on a black woman and another false rumor of a rape of a white woman. Twenty-five black people were killed, many by police and National Guard. Seven hundred people were injured and $2 million worth of property was destroyed.

1985: THE PHILADELPHIA FIREBOMBING OF MOVE

After a daylong confrontation with a radical black-liberation group called MOVE, the Philadelphia police dropped a bomb on the West Philadelphia row house that the MOVE members lived in, killing eleven people, including five children. The fire caused by the police bombing destroyed sixty-five houses in the neighborhood. Two hundred people were made homeless. Nobody involved ever faced any repercussions—not the mayor, not the police.

These are people who were *bombed* in 1985. *In America.*

AN APOLOGY FOR LYNCHING

So fine, maybe we'll never get reparations for being slaves. But what about the violence and lynching directed at us? After slavery ended, it's not as if the former white supremacists who ran the place welcomed black folks to the lunch counter.

According to researchers from Tuskegee University, more than 4,700 people were lynched between 1882 and 1968. That's 4,700 people killed in the reimposition of white terror, especially in the South. And almost none of the perpetrators of that violence were brought to justice, nor were their victims' families compensated in any way.

In 2020, mob lynching still isn't a federal crime. It was only at the end of 2018 that Senators Kamala Harris, Cory Booker, and Tim Scott got their Justice for Victims of Lynching Act of 2018 passed. The Senate had previously failed to pass federal antilynching legislation two hundred times. At the time of the act's passage, Republican senator Cindy Hyde-Smith of Mississippi was the presiding officer; this was the same lady who said she'd be in the front row of a "public hanging" if invited. And even though the House has approved a version of this bill, President Trump has yet to sign it into law.

So the Senate has been slow to recognize the damage done by lynching. Maybe we shouldn't hold our breath for an apology or a payout. But then again, Italians got both.

That's right: the U.S. government paid $25,000 in reparations for Italian Americans who were lynched. Now granted, this was in 1892, but still, $25,000 could buy you a lot of wagons in 1892. And, hey: that's $25,000 more than the United States has paid to us.

You see, in 1891, a mob broke into a New Orleans prison and murdered eleven Italian Americans whom they blamed for the death of the police chief. You have to remember that at the time, Italians were considered basically almost niggas. People in New Orleans did *not* like Italians. People felt like they were taking "American jobs," and Italian immigrants were discriminated against for their darker complexions. Sound familiar?

When the New Orleans police chief, David Hennessy, was killed in an ambush, rumors spread that he had blamed Italians in his dying breath. Hundreds of Italians were arrested, and nineteen people were indicted. None of these people were convicted of the crime, but eleven were lynched by the mob that broke into the prison. The payment of reparations was made to Italy, to distribute to the families affected. As the *New York Times* quoted the secretary of state in 1892: "While the injury was not indicted directly by the United States, the President nevertheless feels that it is the solemn duty as well as the great pleasure of the National Government to pay a satisfactory indemnity. Moreover, the President's instructions carry with them the hope that the transaction of today may efface all memory of the unhappy tragedy."

How is it that President Benjamin Harrison was more enlightened in 1892 than President Trump is in 2020?

And you know how white people hold a grudge. How when they get irritated, they yell "HEY" and startle you. When white people feel irritated, they go looking for an apology and usually get it. So when Michael Santo of the Order Sons and Daughters of Italy in America asked the City of New Orleans for an apology this past year, Mayor LaToya Cantrell decided it was the right thing to do. "At this late date, we cannot give justice, but we can be intentional and deliberate about what we do going forward," said Mayor Cantrell. She asked the crowd "to be the kind of people that our children are not apologizing for 128 years from now."

There's something fucked up about a LaToya apologizing

for a lynching, right? Why is it always up to black people to do the right thing?

So our history books and yours don't match up. What you've done is you've co-opted truth. These false notions get stuck over time and are never challenged. According to my history classes, we didn't do anything but invent the peanut. I mean, the only black person I ever learned about in school was George Washington Carver. You know how hard it was during Black History Month, learning all the aspects of one motherfucker for twenty-eight days? *Wow, normally I like Skippy, but all this history has made me think about checking out Jif.*

So of course you believe we were always slaves and that we didn't do anything else. This country has heard only one side of the story. And then people don't ever want to go back and fix it. We just stop talking about that part of the story because it makes white people uncomfortable. They think we just go right from slavery to playing basketball.

WE SHALL ENDEAVOR TO UNDERSTAND ONE ANOTHER

HISTORY TODAY

So you can understand why we don't understand each other. There's a long history of "misunderstandings." But because we've had these separate histories, here we are today trying to understand each other without a common language.

History is history, but it's also today.

WHY DIDN'T YOU TELL US YOU WERE UNHAPPY?

A lot of old white people agree with what one weird old reality TV star said about the "good old days." No, not *Trump*—the *Duck Dynasty* dude, Phil Robertson. He reminisced about the old days in an interview with *GQ:*

> I never, with my eyes, saw the mistreatment of any black person. Not once. Where we lived was all farmers. The blacks worked for the farmers. I hoed cotton with them. I'm with the blacks, because we're white trash. We're going across the field. . . . They're singing and happy. I never heard one of them, one black person, say, "I tell you what: These doggone white people"—not a word! . . . Pre-entitlement, pre-welfare, you say: Were they happy? They were godly; they were happy; no one was singing the blues.

Why didn't you tell us you were unhappy? You seemed so happy! Never mind that the difference between Phil Robertson, white trash cotton-picker, and any black person in the South was that nobody was trying to lynch Phil Robertson or beat him or prevent him from voting.

Phil Robertson was born in 1946, but even then there was a big difference between white sharecroppers and black sharecroppers. The difference between white trash and niggas is niggas didn't have employees. You know what I'm saying? You can't be that poor when poorer people are working for *you*.

Why does he think they called their music "the blues"? It's called the blues for a reason. White people didn't have the blues before we came along. And singing don't mean you're happy. One of Billie Holiday's signature songs was "Strange Fruit":

Southern trees bear a strange fruit,
Blood on the leaves and blood at the root,
Black body swinging in the Southern breeze,
Strange fruit hanging from the poplar trees.

Maybe white people like Phil Robertson wouldn't hear that this was a song about lynchings. It's a protest song. Black people working out in the fields as slaves used songs as a way to keep themselves connected as a community and to communicate with one another. Songs like "Follow the Drinking Gourd" and "Go Down Moses" contained coded messages. "Follow the Drinking Gourd" refers to the north star and a route to escape. Songs were very subversive; they weren't always happy. They could teach and provide information that white masters wouldn't detect or understand. Black people sang work songs and spirituals to bond. They sang songs when they revolted too. These songs weren't all songs of joy and happiness. They were "When Israel was in Egypt's land, let my people go." They weren't "Sunday, Monday, happy days."

THE GOOD OLD DAYS

So it's really only white people waxing poetic about "the good old days." Because black people don't really have them. When we talk about "the good old days" it's generally the time before we knew we were black. Or it might be "Oh, the good old days were when my dad and mom were together," but there's not a cultural "good old days" for us.

The only reason there used to be a Black Wall Street before it was burned down was because no one would do business with us and we couldn't live anywhere else. So we don't have "good old days," but we do have "kind of good days."

If a black man could use a time machine, he would go

back to 2008. "The good old days" are that recent. Our time machine wouldn't waste no gas. It wouldn't waste no fuel at all.

Beep-beep—"Oh, we're here already? It seems like just yesterday"—it was. Because the further we go back, *the further we go back.*

Take the 1950s. White people are so nostalgic for the 1950s. Isn't that the Great America that we're all supposed to be Making Again? But it's a Great White America.

IHOP recently had a promotion celebrating the "Panniversary" of its founding in 1958. You could get fifty-eight-cent short stacks of pancakes while enjoying a retro menu. As the restaurant's Facebook page promised: "We don't just have 1950s prices, we've got 1950s lingo too. So cruise on through, daddy-o. It's gonna be the bees' knees. The cats' pajamas. Totally aces."

Cute, right? But don't they realize that in the 1950s, I couldn't eat at their restaurant? Let's get real about the 1950s! If you're going to serve up fifty-eight-cent pancakes, they should also come with a waitress who says, "No colored served here." I would rather pay eight dollars for my Rooty Tooty Fresh 'N Fruity and keep the progress. Because a nigga would have to eat in the alley. So, no thanks—I don't want to go back to the '50s. The prices were lower, but so was the tolerance.

LIMITATIONS OF STATUES

So forgive us if we don't want to walk down memory lane with you. History means different things to you and me. Just look at how much time we've spent arguing about statues, especially ones of Confederate war "heroes." White people like to pretend that it's important to keep these statues up, to not "lose history." But a lot of these statues were put up in black neighborhoods during the Jim Crow era. Isn't it strange that they decided just at that moment to start "preserving history"?

The only reason we're able to live freely is because those motherfuckers on the horses lost. So, to you, it's part of your heritage. To me, that's the motherfucker who was so inept, I'm free.

How many statues of Robert E. Lee do you want? Is it worth killing people over? A young woman was murdered in Charlottesville just because people were so worked up about a statue of a Confederate general put up in 1924.

Let's put it this way: if you have to Google who a statue is, you weren't that attached to it. You really still want that statue of the guy who led a charge in 18-whatever where everybody was killed but him in the Battle of Who Cares? Don't pretend it's your favorite statue and that you can't live without it. If I cover your eyes and you can't remember whether it was General Nathaniel Bartholomew Hayes or Corporal Hayworth Bartholomew Nathan, that statue can go.

At least in Philly, they got a statue of Rocky. Everybody knows Rocky. That's a fun statue. That's an Instagrammable statue. I guarantee you more people know Rocky than Nathan Bedford Forrest.

It's pretty safe to say that when you see a bronze statue, you know it's of someone who didn't like black people. I've never seen a bronze statue yet of someone who liked black people. Maybe we shouldn't make statues out of bronze; maybe it's not the people who are racist, it's that alloy.

Let's stop making bronze statues: it's expensive and maybe racist. Why do we gotta keep all these statues forever anyway? Let's make statues out of something easy to get rid of. Statues should be temporary, like your emotions. If you're feeling so excited about someone that you want to put a statue up, you should put it up in something easy to knock down in case you change your mind. You know? It's like a tattoo: you don't get a tattoo for every girl you go out with. You might love somebody one day, but then things change . . .

That's why we propose a time limit on statues. A statue of limitations. I mean a Statute of Statue Limitations. We gotta limit statues, is what I mean.

Let's call it seven years. Seven years per statue, then you have to re-up. That way no one statue gets too comfortable clogging up a park where people don't want it anymore. After seven years, give another statue a chance!

Reparations Article 3a. Statute of Statue Limitations

White people having gotten overly attached to bronze statues of racists, and having erected statues anywhere they could in an effort to remind black people of who was in charge, now agree to end the practice of erecting new bronze statues. Bronze, a possibly racist alloy, will be replaced as a building material by plaster of Paris, Play-Doh, or some other temporary building material. New statues will be limited to a seven-year erection, which is more than you need anyway, in most instances.

And if you want to add more statues, we have to limit new ones and get rid of old ones. We know white people hate quotas, but don't you think that there are too many bronze statues of Confederates? Be reasonable. I'm not advocating for a statue affirmative action policy, but I am advocating for more diversity of statues. We gotta make some room.

Think of all the fun statues we can put up, knowing that we won't have to look at them forever. It's 2020 while I'm writing this, so let's put up a statue of Lil Nas X—what the hell, if that shit doesn't seem right in a few years, we'll just take it down.

BUT WHAT THE HECK, GO AHEAD AND KEEP BLACKFACE

It's weird how much white people like to wear blackface. You all like blackface about as much as you like statues. It feels like every politician who lived through the '70s and '80s dressed up in blackface for their yearbook photo. There are a lot of contenders for "Most Likely to Resign in Disgrace."

The latest example was Ralph Northam, the governor of Virginia, who was about to resign because a picture of him in blackface turned up. At first, he apologized for the picture from his 1984 med school yearbook, but then he said he couldn't be sure that it was really him. Then he changed his mind again. "It was definitely not me," he said at a news conference. "I can tell by looking at it." He was also pretty sure that he wasn't the guy dressed up in the KKK outfit standing next to the dude in blackface.

He could explain: "That same year, I did participate in a dance contest in San Antonio in which I darkened my face as part of a Michael Jackson costume." So he knew that it wasn't him in blackface because he had used shoe polish a different time to look like Michael Jackson. It's weird because in the '80s Michael Jackson was whiter than him. Michael was so white he used to confuse black people: *How does this white woman know how to moonwalk?*

And Northam isn't the only one to have a blackface problem. In the last few years, many different candidates for office around the country have had old blackface pictures turn up. Mississippi governor Tate Reeves and his frat brothers were dressed in blackface and Confederate flags in his 1995 yearbook. Michael Ertel, Florida's secretary of state, resigned because of pictures of him wearing blackface and a "Katrina Victim" T-shirt. And that was from 2005.

Some white people think that photos like this are just youthful mistakes and shouldn't be disqualifying. I mean, haven't we all worn a racist costume now and again in the 1980s? Or in the '90s? Or in 2015?

We won't make you feel bad for all the poor choices you made in the '80s and '90s. That was a long time ago and we all wore some weird shit back then. We'll stop bringing up blackface if you don't bring up our parachute pants and high-top fades.

I think that if you want to dress in blackface, that's fine. If being black appeals to you, go ahead and wear the blackface. But I think the minute you do, your credit score should go down and your blood pressure should go up.

And if white people want to dress in blackface on Halloween, we should have Halloween be on Election Day, so they don't count your vote either.

Reparations Article 3b. Blackface for White Folks

White people, having embraced blackface as a fun dress-up tool, having enjoyed Halloween parties in the 1980s, having engaged in racist skits during fraternity parties of the 1990s, and having celebrated such problematic frivolity by documenting blackface in uncountable yearbook pages, shall henceforth be held blameless. Their love of Michael Jackson is hereby affirmed, and their right to wear blackface is retained. This privilege is restricted, however, to Election Day, bank loan interviews, and any other occasion where historical discrimination against people of color has been exhibited.

BBQ BECKYS

You don't have to wear blackface or a hood to be part of white supremacy's legacy. That's a thing white people don't always understand—they think, just like Trump, that they "don't have a racist bone in their bodies." So why are they always calling the cops on black people for selling water, or having a barbecue?

These days we're living with each other with greater frequency. White people are living near black people where there didn't used to be any white people. Because of gentrification, all of a sudden you have this clash of cultures.

I'll admit: Black people have always done things a little outside the lines. Like opening up a fire hydrant, or climbing up on a pole to steal cable. You know, little things. And for a white person, new to the neighborhood, they're not used to seeing these things, and it's an affront to their sense of justice.

Take BBQ Becky herself: She called the cops on people barbecuing in Oakland at Lake Merritt. People are always barbecuing there, and her outsized beef with a group of black people trying to enjoy their day has everything to do with both gentrification and white people's feeling that they can police black people.

First, she came up and harassed them about being in "her park," then she told them they couldn't have a *charcoal* grill there. Apparently, the grill was in one of several barbecue areas, but this one was for *non-charcoal* grills. Even so, I mean, what the hell? It's in a barbecue area, people are always grilling there. Yeah, it might technically be illegal, but I'm not feeling ready to go up here and arrest all these niggas because they're barbecuing—you'd have to round people up every weekend.

White people are always policing black people. That's why I liked that movie *Bird Box.* In *Bird Box,* there's this force, and if you actually see it, it shows you your greatest fears and sorrows and makes you kill yourself. It's the first thing that I've ever seen that can make white people mind their business. Finally, something to stop you from looking out the window at us. *What is this nigger doing?* I'd welcome that *Bird Box* force into our neighborhoods. And it wouldn't affect black people because we never see anything anyway. *What happened? I didn't see nothing.*

There's so many white ladies calling the cops on black folks, we're running out of names: we got BBQ Becky, Permit Patty, Cornerstore Caroline, Pool Patrol Paula, and a whole lot of others—all trying to regulate black people and using the police to do so. Even if some of the people calling the police aren't racist-bone-having racists, they're not thinking through how police encounters can go bad. Eric Garner got choked out for selling loose cigarettes, not for robbing a bank.

Misunderstandings can happen, of course. Everyone gets things wrong. My housekeeper's been with us for twenty-five years. She came right from Guatemala. We love her, so my wife made her a big meal for Cinco de Mayo and she's like, "I'm Guatemalan." So?

Cinco de Mayo is just for Mexicans, turns out. I guess now we have to cook another big dinner for Día de la Asunción, which is fucked up because cooking is my housekeeper's job.

So how do we get to understanding each other better? I think we probably need better writers. Because when

I look at the LGBTQ community, shows like *Ellen* and *Will & Grace* really changed people's opinions about gay people. Suddenly gay people felt familiar, not threatening. Straight people got to know gay characters whom they liked and could laugh at. Maybe we can talk to the people who write for *Queer Eye.* Because none of them got hanged or assassinated, not even that one guy, Antoni, who doesn't even know how to cook. *Queer Eye for the Black Guy? Black Eye for the White Guy?* Not sure that works, but I'd like to see the way a bunch of black guys fixed up some dude's apartment.

Reparations Article 3c. Black Eyes for the White Guy

It is thus decided, Hollywood's top writers and producers must be brought together in pursuit of a relatable black comedy or makeover show for the masses. We need some of that creativity put in service of making people like us more. We want some shit on Netflix, on NBC, heck, even something that can run on CBS to catch some old white people after *NCIS*.

JUST DON'T CALL ME THE N-WORD WHILE I'M EATING

Still, some white people *do* need to scale back the overt racist shit.

Like, I never understood how Papa John could be racist, because it's black people who keep him in business. He gets on a conference call and says "nigger." And then tries to defend himself? All these fast-food places depend on black people. If you serve shitty food at low prices, niggas buy it. How are you racist to *me*? White people do not eat Papa John's.

And Buffalo Wild Wings had an incident recently where a bunch of black people were told to move because this racist dude didn't want to sit next to niggers, which is ridiculous. Because anytime you have wings, it's like the fucking Field of Dreams: *If you build it, they will come.* You thought you could be at a restaurant with wings and black people wouldn't show up? It's a self-fulfilling prophecy. How the fuck are you gonna get hoity-toity at Wild Wings, motherfucker?

So just don't call me a nigger while I'm eating, all right?

I'm not calling for a boycott; I'm not saying we're going to stop eating your shit. I'm saying we are going to keep eating it, a lot. Just . . . be respectful. Just don't be racist to me while I'm eating. Because, trust me, if I keep like this, I won't be at your restaurant long anyhow. If I'm gonna lose my arm and my eye to diabetes so that you can get rich, at least be nice to my face.

Reparations Article 3d. Don't Call Me the N-Word While I'm Eating

Racism has no place in America, and certainly not in a Buffalo Wild Wings or a Papa John's. Herewith, black people shall eat in peace, without having to deal with slurs and antagonism. Polite dinner conversation only, please.

Plus, you don't want to get rid of us. Because white people never believe in racism unless it's them getting denied a position or a school admission. They don't believe in racism until they're in the unusual position of being on the flip side of the coin. But you need us: you need us to have somebody to blame shit on.

If you live in these really homogenous enclaves with no black people, who can you blame for your problems? If you have a high drug problem, but it's all broke white people, who you gonna blame? If your average-ass kids can't get into an elite school, don't look at me. You need us!

FROM MY COLD, DEAD HANDS

Black people love Buffalo Wild Wings. White people love shootin' things.

Owning a gun is really a "white thing." There's a reason you only see white guys standing around at rallies with assault rifles. Guns are linked to white identity now, not black identity. The Second Amendment doesn't really apply to us.

I live in California, which has the strictest gun laws in the country. It didn't used to be so strict, but in 1967, thirty Black Panthers occupied the California statehouse with shotguns, .357 Magnums, and pistols.

See, "gun rights" are just another thing that white people copied off of black people. It was the Black Panthers who first advocated for gun rights; not so they could go around shooting people, but to protect themselves from a racist government and police force. Bobby Seale, one of the leaders of the Panthers, read a statement that day at the state capitol:

The Black Panther party for self-defense calls upon the American people in general and the black people in particular to take careful note of the racist California Legislature which is considering legislation aimed at keeping the black people disarmed and powerless at the very same time that racist police agencies throughout the country are intensifying the terror, brutality, murder and repression of black people.

After that, Ronald Reagan and the NRA did something they had never done before. They went, "You know what? Did we say Second Amendment? Well, how about a second thought—niggers with guns in the statehouse? I don't think that's what the Founders had in mind." So they passed the Mulford Act, repealing open carry in California.

That's why now a white guy walking into a Walmart with an assault rifle is a "patriot," but a black guy walking into Walmart with an assault rifle is a "target."

Maybe you can't fix everyone's heart, but you can probably make it harder for him to get an AR-15. Unfortunately, white people won't let that happen. They need *protection*. But you know who the most likely person to get killed by a mass shooter is? Another white guy. So for every Dylann Roof who plans out a specifically racially motivated attack, there's another white guy popping off indiscriminately. All those people who got shot in Vegas: Who were they? A bunch of country music fans. The only black people at a country music festival were cleaning up the grounds.

But still, white folks want to hold on to their assault rifles. They won't change the gun laws even though their "independence" and "freedom" are getting them killed. And every time there's a shooting, it's treated like an aberration. Everything is blamed but guns. I saw somebody blame mass shootings on *Call of Duty*. Blaming mass shootings on *Call of Duty* is like blaming our obesity problem on *Pac-Man*.

If you're collecting ammunition and guns, you're not a good guy. You're a bad guy waiting to happen. You're waiting for the end of the world, for a race war, or for the black helicopters to come take your land. Most people don't stockpile weapons in anticipation that Jesus is coming back. You don't need guns for the Rapture. If you're being raptured, guns aren't going to help you where you're going.

And for the privilege of owning these guns, white people are dying. Not from mass shootings and not from gang violence. President Trump and the Right like to make a big deal about how dangerous the inner cities are. Like how in July 2019 Trump tweeted about Representative Elijah Cummings's district in Baltimore, calling it a "very dangerous & filthy place."

But the majority of gun deaths in America are white men committing suicide. Approximately twenty-five thousand Americans kill themselves with guns each year. So it's this "protection" that's killing white people. When it comes to guns, you all should be a bit more like us black folk.

LET'S BE APPROPRIATE

It's weird when I see a black woman with a blond wig and blue contacts complain about cultural appropriation. That's a little strange. It's a complicated topic. But we can't talk about cultural appropriation and then invite somebody over for spaghetti.

I think anytime you have cultural intermingling, there are gonna be natural kinds of exchanges. Like some of the stuff we eat, we got from you. I know a lot of black folks think we invented everything, but it's not *totally* true. We all sing each other's songs, shit like that.

So I think that we're gonna have to let you off the hook for "cultural appropriation." Because I don't think all of us wanna go back to looking like we did in the '70s. We've all been stealing from each other long enough that I think it'll be too hard to sort it all out. If we're gonna fuck with white musicians who sound like niggas, then we're also gonna have to tell Mom to stop making her "great macaroni and cheese."

So if you all just accept Lil Nas X, I won't have to give up Hall and Oates, you know? We'll call this a draw. In return, we'll stop complaining when a Kardashian puts braids in her hair. Deal?

Reparations Article 3e. We Keep Mac and Cheese and Hall and Oates

Lest the foodstuffs and music much adored by all peoples become the subject of continuous wrangling and conflict, we heresoforwith declare cultural appropriation to be approved for use by all peoples. Just don't be a big jerk about it.

WHITE PEOPLE CAN'T JUST SAY SHIT

That doesn't mean that white people can just say shit.

Maybe, if we're lucky, Trump will have been imprisoned by the time this book comes out. But in the lead-up to an impeachment inquiry, Trump tweeted out:

So some day, if a Democrat becomes President and the Republicans win the House, even by a tiny margin, they can impeach the President, without due process or fairness or any legal rights. All Republicans must remember what they are witnessing here—a lynching. But we will WIN!

A *lynching*. No one should expect Trump to be careful with his words, but he's symptomatic of how white people act like they're the victims. You gotta stop comparing yourself to black people when it's convenient for you. Trump: You ain't black. You orange.

Impeachment is a political remedy that the Founding Fathers put there for a reason. It's like an emergency exit that's available if we need it. They wanted to make sure that if there were high crimes and misdemeanors, we weren't permanently stuck with a president. They were concerned about people using the levers of government to enrich themselves or to oppress somebody and get away with all kinds of malfeasance. An impeachment is carried out by men and women in suits and it's very official. A lynching is where mobs come and string you up.

Four thousand seven hundred people were lynched between 1882 and 1968. Only three presidents have been impeached. And none of them has actually ever been convicted by the Senate and removed from office. So there's a difference in kind and scale. It's actually nothing like lynching.

So you gotta stop comparing yourself to black people when it's convenient for you. You can't quote Martin Luther King Jr. when you've just said the most racist shit ever.

So you're banned. You lose the ability to play the black card when you think it works for you.

HELP YOURSELF

I don't want you to do any of this stuff just because it's right or because you feel bad. Don't do it to help us. When black people get anything, it invariably benefits white people more. Help yourself!

Take affirmative action. Tucker Carlson equated it to Jim Crow:

> The other factor that colleges don't like to talk about is affirmative action. The Supreme Court banned the use of racial quotas in admissions some years ago, but in real life, that decision meant nothing. Skin color remains a central consideration at every level of the process. The average admissions office is every bit as

race conscious as any institution in the Jim Crow South, and far less transparent about it.

    —Tucker Carlson Tonight, *April 18, 2018*

Perfect example. Affirmative action helped white women more than it helped us. More women became part of the workplace due to affirmative action than black people. It increased their access to contracts and jobs that were closed to them before. And that's still true. Affirmative action primarily benefits white women, so don't get rid of it! Help yourself!

Or welfare. When Trump met with members of the Congressional Black Caucus, after he made sure everyone had met Ben Carson, he was taken to task by a congresswoman about proposed welfare cuts. She told him that the cuts would harm her constituents, "not all of whom are black." Trump replied: "Really? Then what are they?"

That's typical of Republicans who hate welfare, food stamp programs, and benefits for poor people. With nearly every budget proposal, they attack these programs. But when they do things thinking that they're embarrassing us or taking us down a notch, it hurts white people. In 2018, the Trump administration sought a 20 percent reduction to spending on SNAP. When they do that shit, it hurts

Walmart more than black people. In 2017, $33 billion of SNAP benefits were spent at big-box stores like Walmart and Target.

So don't be so quick to cut shit. You better keep welfare, not because you like us, but because you want to help yourself!

Any "handout" invariably helps you more. Whatever you give us, you get to steal anyway. Who knows, maybe you all will get some reparations too . . .

WHITE PEOPLE DON'T LIKE TO FEEL BAD

The fact of the matter is that white people are always uncomfortable talking about race. They don't want to talk about race—they like *not* talking about it. Because in the end, white people don't want to feel bad.

An extreme example of this is the review left by a couple who felt upset during their tour of Whitney Plantation, which explicitly bills itself as "the only plantation museum in Louisiana with an exclusive focus on the lives of enslaved people." Leaving a two-star review, the couple complained that the tour guide made them feel bad:

> My husband and I were extremely disappointed in this tour. We didn't come to hear a lecture on how

the white people treated slaves, we came to get this history of a southern plantation and get a tour of the house and grounds. The tour guide was so radical about slave treatment we felt we were being lectured and bashed about the slavery. My ancestors were from Sicily, never owned slaves, and my husbands were German, and none of his ever owned slaves. I am by far not racist or against all Americans having equal rights but this was my vacation and now we are crossing all plantation tours off our list, it was just not what we expected. I'll go back to Louisiana and see some real plantations that are so much more enjoyable to tour.

You don't even want to feel bad about slavery on a tour of enslaved people's quarters? You felt "lectured and bashed about the slavery" on your vacation? Maybe you need to reflect a bit on your expectations. History is allowed to make you uncomfortable. I just have one suggestion for this couple: Cancel your honeymoon trip to Auschwitz. Florida can be nice.

Also, as we've seen before: Are you *sure* that none of your ancestors owned slaves? Believe it or not, some of the people who owned slaves were from Italy, some from Germany.

People always act like it could never have been possible. *My ancestors never owned slaves.* Well, somebody's ancestors did! Who were these owners if they weren't Germans and Italians and Irish? Who were they? "Oh, I'm from Scandinavia." You can't all be from Scandinavia.

White people don't know our history, and they willfully ignore it. Steve King, a Republican congressman from Iowa, said that black people never contributed anything to society or civilization: "I would ask you to go back through history and figure out where are these contributions that have been made by these other categories of people you are talking about [nonwhite people]. Where did any other subgroup of people contribute more to civilization?" You know, not math or plumbing or astronomy or science or agriculture. None of that. I guess that all started from Iowa, just outside of Jerusalem.

But it's easy to feel that way about people when you're so ill-informed about who they are and where they came from. Because, in truth, America's point of reference for black people is slavery. To white people, our story started with enslavement, with us being here in chains. So that's the thing: The African American story starts in the middle. Never at the beginning.

Here's our offer: We'll pretend like we don't know the

things we know. We agree to participate in this selective amnesia with you. And because history and Google are incompatible, we hereby move to Bing for all web searches.

Reparations Article 3f. Bing Only

In consideration of Google's accurate search results, which serve only to dredge up true, horrible, unpleasant facts that make white people feel bad, all black people are hereby sentenced to use Bing only for searches, so that the information is less true, less accurate, and less painful.

YOU PRETEND TO LIKE BLACK PEOPLE

You pretend to like black people, but you don't treat us with respect or kindness. It just feels like when white people talk about black people, it's never about love. It's always about *tough love*. Never *love* love. Why is that?

It always comes from a place of discipline and bringing the hammer down. It's never about understanding or empathy. It's always about correcting defects, always about bringing black people to heel.

WE GET TO BE AVERAGE

We're always judged by the exception, not the rule. Everybody always goes, "Why can't you be like Michael Jordan?" But there are fourteen other people on that team. And guess what? None of them are Michael Jordan either.

Or: "Why can't you be like Barack Obama? He did it. He was raised by a single mother and he went to school, got educated, and became president. Why can't you do it?"

Do you know how much good karma and kismet you need to get through the maze? With the obstacles of discrimination and history, you have to celebrate the success stories but not pretend they're the norm or act like nobody else has to be exceptional to succeed. We're always held up to the exception, as opposed to the rule.

The rule is that you should be able to make a living just being mediocre. It should be okay to be average. Look at all the average white men who made it. Take Donald Trump: Donald Trump is very average.

Even with every advantage, think of how many average white folks there are like Donald Trump. They had better schools, more resources, more money, and the ultimate luxury: being allowed to be average and have it work out. That's all we want: to be able to be average, to make a decent living and live a safe, average life. As it is, we have to be exceptional and you get to be average. But if we fail, if we have a hard time because the obstacles were too great, you blame *us* and say, "Well, we tried."

> ## Reparations Article 3g. We Get to Be Average
>
> Until such a time as the number of average black folks equals the number of average white folks in positions of power, acclaim, and wealth, black people shall herewith be allowed to be "normal," "average," and "unremarkable" without being deemed deficient. Until such a time as the amount of "remarkable" white people in charge of things, held up for praise, or otherwise regarded as successful increases, black people shall enjoy the same respect for being average as their white peers, suffering no penalty.

And anyway, society doesn't like strong black people. They didn't like Martin Luther King Jr. till he was dead, right? They didn't like Muhammad Ali till he was holding the Olympic torch. Remember? He was shaking so bad, people went and blew their pilot lights out. Like, "This motherfucker ain't blowing my house up."

WE GET TO PICK THE BLACK PEOPLE

That's not to say you don't like *any* black folk. You do. You just don't like the ones we like. So for the purposes of this treaty and just to be clear: we get to pick the black people. Y'all have forfeited the right to pick. Because we know how you like to play it: you like to pick weak and unremarkable black people. If we let white people pick black people, we know what we'll get.

Whenever Republicans need a black person, they always pick someone unremarkable. Name me one black man they'll ever pick who will have a street or a library named after him. We can go down the list. Need a black guy for the Supreme Court? Don't worry, you've got Clarence Thomas—totally unremarkable. You already fill thirteen of your sixteen cabinet slots with white guys, so you need a black guy to run Housing and Urban Development? After all, it says "urban" right in the title. Why not take former brain surgeon Ben Carson? Trump even tried to put Herman Cain, a pizza chain mogul, into the Federal Reserve.

Ben Carson, Clarence Thomas, and Herman Cain are

remarkable only in how much they are unremarkable. And you never see them at the same time. That's weird, right?

Sometimes I think I'm being unfair to Ben Carson. I mean, supposedly he's a bright guy. Sure, it's weird to have a neurosurgeon without any housing policy experience run a huge housing agency like HUD. That's crazy. But maybe if you're bright it doesn't matter; a bright guy could look at the problems of HUD and say, "This is fair, this is not fair." Maybe chopping into brains is just like chopping into budgets, I don't know.

Isn't that the Republican argument all the time? Those analytic skills should translate to something new. That's why Trump's supposed to be good at being president—because he's a genius businessman. Or Rex Tillerson should be a good secretary of state because he ran Exxon. Success at one thing should be able to be applied to something else. Indeed, it's *more* valuable than expertise in a given field.

But tell me, if Ben Carson's so bright, how come he went before Maxine Waters's Financial Services Committee and didn't know what "REO" stood for? Now, granted, I didn't know that it stood for "real-estate owned," but I'm not HUD secretary. This is his job!

Representative Katie Porter asked him, "Do you know what an REO is?"

"An Oreo?" Carson replied. An *Oreo*? He thought he was being insulted. He thought she was calling him an Oreo. I bet he's heard that before. And then instead of admitting he didn't know what he was talking about, he got mad and acted arrogant. If a black man talked back to the cops the way he talked to the committee, Republicans would not cheer. They would advocate for him being shot or tased.

So what is that about? That's about desire. He doesn't care about HUD; he doesn't care about learning his job. Either he's not as bright as they say he is or he's a lazy brilliant person. If you are intelligent, it should travel. Some of that intelligence should have followed you. Maybe he's a brain surgeon like Donald Trump is a business tycoon.

And why doesn't Clarence Thomas ever say anything? Clarence Thomas decided to shut up to show people: he didn't want to sound stupid, so he stopped talking. "It's better to be silent and thought a fool, than to speak and remove all doubt."

Donald Trump and the Republicans of this ilk like black people the same way they like their dogs: obedient. *Slap me five and don't shit on the carpet.*

All this is to say: we get to pick the black people.

But since you guys love him so much, you can have Kanye. We're tired of him.

> ### *Reparations Article 3h. Take Kanye*
>
> Kanye is yours. He's an honorary white guy now. Since he likes to hang out with Trump so much and spout a bunch of crazy nonsense all the time, we trade him to you.

Since we're picking our own black folks, let's make some trades to keep it simple. We'll give you some black people and you can give us some white people.

Unfortunately, there's probably only three white people we like. One is Gary Owen. Come on over, Gary. Two is that dude who plays Tommy on *Power*. Three is . . . Michael something. He's a white scholar, and niggas quote him all the time. You know the guy . . . Look, I'll send out a final list later. Oh, and Teena Marie too. Like how the Mormons can baptize dead people, we'll convert her to black posthumously. She's dope.

And in return, you can have Kanye, you can have Candace Owens. You can have Ben Carson and Herman Cain too. You can have Diamond and Silk, you can have Stacey Dash, you can have any of them shoe-bootie creatures.

And this isn't just about trading famous white people for famous black people. We want to help poor white people too. Mortality rates for virtually every group have been dropping over time for the last hundred years. But for poor, uneducated whites, the mortality rate is going up. You can't attribute this to war or famine; the increase is because whiteness ain't enough.

Poor white people are under the illusion that they're like the rich white people they see on TV, but they're not. With no jobs, no support system, they can't deal with the fact that they aren't getting what they were promised from the American Dream. They're supposed to be in charge, respected and revered. Instead, they're ignored and forgotten. That strain, that disconnect, is making them do drugs, commit suicide, and drink themselves to death. The Blue Book value on "white" just ain't what it was.

But we can't have that. After all, this state of affairs gave us Trump. So we will take your poor white people and teach them how to adjust. We'll make them niggas for free. Since we have so much in common, we'll grandfather all you poor white people in and make you honorary black people. So come on—no more killing yourself! We'll teach you how to manage disappointment, poverty, and living with the stress of having rich white people look down on you. I promise that we can turn things around for you. You too can be black!

> ### Reparations Article 31. White Black People
>
> On the condition that you live like a black person but are in all other respects white, if you're forgotten, ignored, disrespected, economically disadvantaged, picked on, and stressed, you are henceforth, for all intents and purposes, a black person.

We get to decide who's black, but also some of these people have tried to jump ship before their time. You know? While we're trading, we can't have some people pretending they're white *already*. I get it, it's inconvenient to be black. But damn—if everyone tries to become white, what the fuck am I negotiating this treaty for? Know what I mean? If everyone is white, including black people, who's gonna sign this thing? I guess that if you could be transracial just like being transgender, then all black people should become white people and then we won't have this problem anymore. Until then, we gotta keep shit sorted.

So there's a few people who *think* they're white or *pretend* they're white, but who are, and shall remain, black:

Like Mike Tirico, the sportscaster. He's such a nigga, it's ridiculous. "Why do I have to check any box?" he said in an interview with the *New York Times*. "If we live in a world where we're not supposed to judge, why should anyone care about identifying?" Okay, you don't have to check the box, I'm checking it for you. Nigga, you be so sub-Saharan. You gotta stay with us.

Reparations Article 3j. If You're Black, You're Black, Unless You're Not

Excluding those already denoted by name (Kanye et al.), if you are black, you are black. No trading in your blackness until we've sorted this whole thing out.

And don't make us revoke your black status. Houston Rockets general manager Daryl Morey tweeted out, "Fight for freedom. Stand with Hong Kong," and the NBA was like, "Hey, man, it's the largest emerging market in the world. We wanna sell our product. Shut up about that freedom shit."

You can't expect the NBA to do the right thing because they're all about making money. But then you heard black people say the same thing. James Harden of the Rockets said, "We apologize. You know, we love China. We love playing there." And then LeBron tweeted: "My team and this league just went through a difficult week. I think people need to understand what a tweet or statement can do to others. And I believe nobody stopped and considered what would happen. Could have waited a week to send it." Right on, LeBron—making money is more important than freedom for the people of Hong Kong?

I mean, I can't imagine black people ever not saying yes to freedom. That's the weirdest shit ever. They can't say yes to freedom because they wanna sell shoes? We wanted freedom and got it. LeBron has been able to build incredible wealth. Then we don't want to talk about freedom for other people because that fucks up the bottom line? That almost makes us white guys.

I mean, freedom to niggas is like catnip. It's our thing! When "freedom" comes up, we gotta chime in. We gotta lead the conversation.

VERY BAD PEOPLE ON BOTH SIDES

We know how you all want us to "cancel" black people when they do something bad, but you keep making excuses for people you revere. People say, "Can we just draw the line at rapists and murderers?" For us, history is rife with horrible men, and then we've learned that we have to sing praises to those horrible men, and we see them on our money and their names on our schools, on our bridges.

So "horrible man" is not a disqualifier. Our lives are imbued with them. When they ask us about Michael Jackson ("How can you sing those songs?") and R. Kelly—it's complicated. I will get rid of Michael Jackson when you get rid of Andrew Jackson. At least you can dance to "Beat It."

But our stories are so full of irredeemably horrible people that it's something that we can compartmentalize. Literally, if Bill Cosby was a priest, he wouldn't be in prison.

TAKE COLUMBUS DAY OFF

But before we get rid of history, let's stop celebrating holidays we know are bullshit. How can you defend Columbus Day? It's like those stupid statues: nobody ever wants to admit that a holiday has outstayed its welcome. It's like we moved, but we already bought the stationery. But come on.

Who really believes nowadays that Christopher Columbus discovered America? No one celebrates it really. One time I had to get to my radio show on a Monday and traffic was so light, it was like the apocalypse. I was like, "Why?" But then it turned out that it was Columbus Day. So thanks to this murdering rapist, I got to work on time.

Think I'm exaggerating or that Columbus wasn't all that bad? I mean, after all, "In 1492 / Columbus sailed the ocean blue" is a pretty cute little rhyme. And what about the *Nina,* the *Pinta,* and the *Santa Maria*? Why the hell was I taught all those ship names if Columbus was really a genocidal maniac?

Historians have firsthand accounts of some of Columbus's worst acts. He forced natives into slavery, to find gold for him. Those who didn't had their hands cut off. He enslaved more than 1,500 people and rewarded his men by allowing them to rape the native women and girls. Columbus himself wrote to a friend, "There are plenty of dealers who go about looking for girls; those from nine to ten are now in demand, and for all ages a good price must be paid." It's estimated that in 1493 there were eight million indigenous people in the Caribbean islands. By the time Columbus left in 1504, there were only about one hundred thousand. Not a good dude.

So we've got Martin Luther King Jr. Day and Columbus Day, and everybody else has to share, huh? So how the hell did it get to be a holiday? Well, weirdly, it has to do with those Italians again! You know, the other black folk who graduated into white folk. As I told you before, Italians were an unpopular bunch of people, especially as their numbers grew in America between 1880 and 1914. Remember how those Italian immigrants got lynched in New Orleans in 1891? Well, a year later, in 1892, President Benjamin Harrison made a proclamation honoring the four hundredth anniversary of Columbus's voyage, in a bid to link Columbus to the great progress America had made since then. This was all part of the plan to smooth things over with the Italian government and signal that Italians *mattered,* and that lynching was wrong (at least for Italians). Italians at the time were thought of as almost black, described in the press as "swarthy" and "kinky-haired" and sometimes as "white niggers." But Italians, seeking to be viewed as Americans in good standing—you know, white people—glommed on to Columbus as a famous Italian to be celebrated. And finally, the Knights of Columbus, a Catholic fraternal organization, pushed President Franklin Delano Roosevelt into declaring Columbus Day a holiday in 1934.

So Columbus started the slave trade and helped a bunch

of Italians stop being niggas. *In 1492 / Columbus sailed the ocean blue / But now in 2019 / Columbus Day is real obscene.* Getting to work on time and buying a mattress—that's all Columbus is good for now. I feel like Columbus's ship has sailed.

And it's weird that all the woke black people who pooh-pooh Columbus Day turn around and then six weeks later celebrate Thanksgiving. That's a little weird. I guess Indians with turkey and cranberries are different.

Now come on, D.L.! Don't fuck with Thanksgiving. We gotta keep this one—I like the football and sometimes even eating with my family.

All right, all right. But the only reason Squanto (his real name was Tisquantum) was around to help the Pilgrims is because he had been kidnapped, shipped off to Europe, and sold into slavery before they had arrived. He knew English because he had lived in London. When he finally got back to his village, everyone had been wiped out by an epidemic that white people had brought over. So enjoy your candied yams, but don't forget that poor Squanto helped a lot of lost white people survive the winter, even though he'd been a slave. We gotta make sure white people get where they're going!

Reparations Article 3k. Personal Days

All holidays must herewith be evaluated as a whole;
i.e., all holidays will be put on a probationary period to
ascertain their relevance and value to all Americans.
Acknowledging that days off are nice and that
mattress sales must occur, a number of holidays shall
be continued, but no current holiday will by reason of
tradition be kept without scrutiny. MLK Day excluded,
because you already tried to take that shit away.

THE GREATEST AMERICANS

The people you admire, the most popular, the most note-
worthy people of the last two hundred years: we know
these motherfuckers have said and done some horrible
stuff. I'm telling you: if we take a look at the greatest
Americans of all time, you'd see that they did some great
shit and some racist shit. That's why we've had to make
allowances; we can't throw out everyone in America, because even the "great" Americans have said horrible things
about us.

We Googled it up (I can't use Bing for this, come on),
and sure enough there was a four-part TV special in 2005

called *The Greatest American,* where millions of people voted for who they thought deserved the title of "Greatest American." Hosted by Matt Lauer, apparently when he wasn't busy harassing women.

So here's the top twenty-five, back in 2005:

25. Neil Armstrong
24. Henry Ford
23. The Wright Brothers
22. Rosa Parks
21. Muhammad Ali
20. Lance Armstrong
19. Eleanor Roosevelt
18. Bill Gates
17. Bob Hope
16. JFK
15. Thomas Edison
14. Albert Einstein
13. Walt Disney
12. Thomas Jefferson
11. Billy Graham
10. FDR
9. Oprah
8. Elvis Presley

7. Bill Clinton

6. George W. Bush

5. Benjamin Franklin

4. George Washington

3. MLK

2. Abraham Lincoln

1. Ronald Reagan

Let's set aside the black folks from the list and also Albert Einstein, because he was born in Germany. Oh, yeah, let's also pull Lance Armstrong, because come on now—the list was made in 2005. But even the fact that he was included is instructive, right? People—probably a lot of white people—voted for *Lance Armstrong* to be in the top twenty-five Greatest Americans over people like Maya Angelou or Frederick Douglass.

So I guarantee you that most of these people said some racist shit. I won't do all of them because by the time we finish the list, Matt Lauer will be accused of raping somebody else, but here are a few examples.

HENRY FORD

He once said: "Don't find fault, find a remedy; anybody can complain."

He also said: "The Jew is a race that has no civilization to point to, no aspiring religion, no great achievement in any form."

FDR

He once said: "The only thing we have to fear is fear itself."

He also interned Japanese Americans and put Hugo Black, a former KKK member, on the Supreme Court.

JFK

He once said: "Ask not what your country can do for you, but what you can do for your country."

He also dropped Sammy Davis Jr. from his inauguration guest list after Davis married a Swedish actress in 1960 because he wanted to keep Southern racists supporting his agenda.

WALT DISNEY

He created Mickey Mouse and Goofy.

He also created *Song of the South* and a racist crow in *Dumbo* literally named "Jim Crow."

THOMAS JEFFERSON

He wrote: "We hold these truths to be self-evident, that all men are created equal, that they are endowed by their Creator with certain unalienable Rights, that among these are Life, Liberty and the pursuit of Happiness."

He also owned more than six hundred slaves, was a rapist, and wrote, "Blacks are in reason much inferior . . . and in imagination they are dull, tasteless, and anomalous . . . never yet could I find that a black had uttered a thought above the level of plain narration."

BILLY GRAHAM

He said: "God has given us two hands, one to receive with and the other to give with."

He also said: "The only hope for enduring peace is Jesus Christ," and "Only when Christ comes again will the little white children of Alabama walk hand in hand with little black children."

ABRAHAM LINCOLN

He said: "Four score and seven years ago our fathers brought forth on this continent a new nation, conceived in liberty, and dedicated to the proposition that all men are created equal." And he freed the slaves.

But he also said: "I will say then that I am not, nor ever have been, in favor of bringing about in any way the social and political equality of the white and black races. . . . And inasmuch as they cannot so live, while they do remain together there must be the position of superior and inferior, and I as much as any other man am in favor of having the superior position assigned to the white race."

RONALD REAGAN

He said: "Mr. Gorbachev, tear down this wall!"

And he also said to Nixon, in talking about UN delegates: "To see those, those monkeys from those African countries—damn them, they're still uncomfortable wearing shoes!"

So even your heroes—the heroes you hold in high esteem—have been instrumental in keeping us where we are. Isn't it funny that the people who the country loves hate us?

BIG LOVE / BIG HATE

And who hates us more than Trump? The president you all chose set out to undo everything Barack Obama did.

Obama cared more about America than he cared about himself. He's the one who put "America First." He epitomized what a president should be. He read the manual and went, "Imma be that." And he did it to the nth degree. You didn't catch him cussing or involved in sex scandals. He was pristine. I mean, obviously he had the kind of small problems that everybody else has; it's a big job. He made a ton of mistakes. But what you can't ever question is that he was very earnest. And he took the weight and the pomp and circumstance seriously—those traditions meant something to him, and the idea of being president meant something to him. He ain't trying to have his personal merchandise in the gift shop and shit. He don't have his own cigarette line. You know what I mean?

That's shit he wasn't gonna do. And that extends up to talking about the current sitting president. He hasn't gone on the talk shows, talking trash about Trump. It'd be so easy for him to do that, especially because Trump has tried to unwind all of Obama's policies. It's long-standing precedent to not bad-mouth your successor and so that's what Obama is going to do, because precedent and high standards are more important to him than scoring political points. He's what a president is supposed to be and now he's what an ex-president is supposed to be.

Obama was the kind of president you always said you wanted. He was the kind of black man you always said you respected, yet you do everything to disrespect him. So how can we take you seriously when you tell us how to be? I find it totally disingenuous: Everything he was was what you told us we had to be. And yet you opposed him at every opportunity and then elected his opposite.

Obama believed in America more than America ever believed in itself, because it had never been challenged. Before Obama, all the presidents looked a certain way. I mean, they might've checked a different box politically, but they all pretty much had the same background: Skull and Bones secret society, blue blood, you know? They were all the same. But he was so different, and he expanded what this country could be.

The first time I can remember black people calling

ourselves "American" was when Barack Obama was in office. Because otherwise, hearing us talk, it sounded like we were describing a place we were visiting. We've always been American, but Obama made us feel like Americans for the first time. He proved that we belong here.

MOST RACIST PRESIDENT

So how can you elect Trump after that? How can you say he's anything but a rejection of everything that Obama represented? Obama made us feel like we belong; Trump makes sure we don't.

According to Pulitzer Prize–winning presidential historian Jon Meacham, Trump ties Andrew Johnson as "the most racist president in American history." And look: that's hard to do. As Meacham describes, Johnson believed "that African-Americans were incapable of self-government and relapsed into barbarism if they weren't closely supervised." So that's pretty stiff competition. The conversation around reparations was stopped under Johnson, but maybe Trump is our opportunity to get it right. When those ministers spoke to God and consulted and came up with "forty acres and a mule," it took a racist president to stop that conversation. Maybe it's like a cycle, now that we have the second-most-racist president.

Now, not everyone agrees that Trump is racist. One of Trump's supporters is New Hampshire state representative Werner Horn. He refused to call slavery racist, claiming that "human beings have been owning other human beings since the dawn of time. It's never been about race." In an interview with *HuffPost*, he clarified that "it's never okay to own another person. But to label the institution as racist is a false narrative." Horn said slave masters weren't considering race but were making "an economic decision" based on who was available. Auction inventory lists simply didn't have "white names," or "Native American" or "Hispanic" names.

Interesting. It's like going to the store and seeing they only have Crest toothpaste. You would have enslaved Aim, but they were out of it. I wonder how so many black people became "available"? And why is it that they only have black people for sale?

If you don't want to call *slavery* racist, then you really don't want to call *anything* racist. I really think that some people only believe you're racist if you say "nigger." But the most racist N-word I've ever heard is "no." No, you can't vote. No, you can't own a home here. No, you can't go to this school.

It shouldn't be too hard to believe that Trump is racist, because he grew up in a racist household. His dad, Fred

Trump, had a long history of racial discrimination in housing. As one of New York City's biggest developers, he was sued for refusing to rent to blacks. In 1967, a state investigation found that of 3,700 apartments in Trump Village, one of Fred Trump's developments, only seven were occupied by blacks. One superintendent testified that he was told to attach a piece of paper with a big letter *C* on it (for "colored") to applications from blacks.

Recently, an article in the *New York Times* from June 1927 was uncovered describing Fred Trump's arrest at a Klan rally in Queens, New York. One thousand Klan members marched in a parade through Jamaica, Queens. After a riot with police, Fred and six other people were arrested. That's not necessarily proof that he was in the Klan; he might have just been an innocent bystander or Klan parade enthusiast.

Of course, President Trump denied that this ever happened: "He was never arrested. He has nothing to do with this. This never happened. This is nonsense and it never happened." Clearly the *New York Times* was already part of the Fake News Conspiracy against Trump as early as 1927.

And half the shit that Trump does, most niggas I know are in jail for. Witness tampering. Intimidation. Lying. Obstructing justice. When Michael Cohen testified, Trump said, "But he should give information maybe on his father-in-law, because that's the one that people want to look at," trying to intimidate him by bringing his family into the matter. And the dudes I know who are in jail weren't even as overt as he is.

Maybe if we're lucky, he'll be in jail by the time this book comes out in paperback.

ARTICLE IV

WE SHALL DEAL WITH THE WHITE SUPREMACY PROBLEM

"WHITE SUPREMACY IS NOT A PROBLEM"

Even if you think Trump isn't racist, he at least exacerbates the white supremacy problem. Everybody knows that the first step to healing is *admitting* you have a problem. But rather than try to address the problem, some on the Right want to deny that there even *is* a problem. According to Fox News's Tucker Carlson, white supremacy is a *hoax:*

But the whole thing is a lie. If you were to assemble a list, a hierarchy of concerns of problems this country faces, where would white supremacy be on the list? Right up there with Russia, probably.

Okay, so I actually *do* think that Russia is a problem, but go on . . .

It's actually not a real problem in America. The combined membership of every white supremacist organization in this country would be able to fit inside a college football stadium. . . . You know, I've lived here fifty years, I've never met anybody—not one person—who ascribes to white supremacy. I don't know a single person who thinks that's a good idea.

Really? Like you never have? You work at Fox, right?

And this was right after a gunman killed twenty-two people in a mass shooting in El Paso, Texas. The shooter posted a racist, xenophobic manifesto online *explicitly* detailing his white supremacist views. Even Ted Cruz tweeted, "What we saw yesterday was a heinous act of terrorism and white supremacy." When a gunman says that he's shooting up a place because of a "Hispanic invasion of Texas," *yeah,* I'd call that a white supremacist.

You'd think after the various mass murders of the last few years, it would be impossible to deny that white supremacy is a problem, but here's a partial list of recent mass shootings by white supremacists:

- The Walmart shooting in El Paso, Texas
- The shooting at a food festival in Gilroy, California
- The shooting at a synagogue in Pittsburgh
- The shooting at a synagogue near San Diego
- The shooting at a supermarket in Kentucky
- And so on (sadly this list will already be out of date by the time you read this) . . .

Now maybe what Tucker meant is that the white supremacy problem isn't a *problem.* And that might seem true; it might not be a problem for white guys like him.

THE REAL WHITE SUPREMACY PROBLEM

My main problem with white supremacy is there's not enough actual *supremacy* in it. What I mean is, where are the *exceptional* people at? You can't be a white supremacist living in a trailer on government assistance. The white supremacists marching in Charlottesville were chanting "You will not replace us." But if you have time to check into a hotel, march for three days, go to a rally, and you didn't take a vacation, you've pretty much been replaced already, right?

I mean, come on, man! You're fucking up the *brand*.

My white supremacy problem is it ain't truth in advertising. Stephen Miller? Steve Bannon? Mitch McConnell? Have you seen these motherfuckers? You wanna continue the white race? Well, you've gotta be able to get laid. Damn, the white supremacists these days look like shit. Nobody looks at Bannon and thinks, *That's a supreme specimen of humanity.*

Didn't there used to be a certain standard? Like an entrance exam or something? If you're gonna claim to be better than the entire rest of humanity, put some effort into it. Keep up appearances at least.

And I get it, you thought it was just gonna be enough to be white, and it ain't anymore. It's a rude awakening. I've always loved America for what it was: the good parts and the ugly, the kindness and the brutality—all of it. White people are just now getting to know the reality, and they don't like it. They don't want to hear about the ugliness; they don't care as long as they can stay feeling good about being white.

But whiteness ain't enough now. You should buy low, sell high, but at a certain point you have to cut your losses. I had this house in Rosemont in L.A. that I bought for $100,000 and it went down to $90,000 and stayed there. I lost some money, but I sold when I could. That's whiteness right now.

The market ain't what it was. Nothing is what it was. Radio is not what it was. TV is not what it was. America is changing, whether you like it or not. We're getting fatter and dumber; the rest of the world is catching up, fast.

JOBS FOR RACISTS

White supremacists are lashing out at the wrong people, convinced that their dwindling economic opportunities are black and brown people's fault. I'm not saying that racists shouldn't have jobs. I'm saying that they shouldn't have jobs where they control other people's fates, like judges or jailers or police officers. I'm not saying they can't be hired for anything. They abuse their positions of power and their views are loathsome, but they're still people.

Maybe some of these racists have skills that can translate

to new jobs. There are a lot of "soft skills" that racists have that employers are looking for:

- **BEING A TEAM PLAYER:** Racists are actually pretty good at being a team, whether it's the Klan or the Republican Party, so maybe they can work together to help a business instead of working together to assemble a torch-carrying mob.

- **FLEXIBILITY:** Racists aren't normally shown respect for their flexibility, but their *moral* flexibility is astonishing, if you think about it. The "moral majority" will wrap themselves up in righteousness, then cheer on a twice-divorced, adulterous liar who cages children like he's the chosen one.

- **EFFECTIVE COMMUNICATION:** Racists have stayed "on message" for the better part of two centuries. And they've proven they can adapt to today's fast-moving media landscape, setting up *Breitbart* and 4chan while retweeting racist memes and repeating Trump's talking points as quickly as they come.

- **DEDICATION:** Racists aren't real good at problem-solving, having been working on the "race" problem for the last few hundred years without success. But they are *persistent*. Effort counts for so much in life, doesn't it?

- **DISCRIMINATING TASTE:** Racists are rightfully regarded for their "discriminating" eye. What if we directed their talents toward more productive ends? Since racists are great at discriminating based on color, maybe they can be put to work in photographic color correction, identifying printing errors, or stoplight testing.

Plus, we want to keep people employed and busy. China and India are breathing down our neck. I'm looking for solutions here. We can't have a bunch of unemployed racists sitting around West Virginia. We've all got to pull our weight.

Reparations Article 4a. Full Employment for Racists

Acknowledging that "idle hands are the devil's playthings," and in consideration of the long history of idle racists stirring up trouble, ascribing their woes to the gainfully employed of other races, all efforts shall be made to keep racists employed, with job training to put their "skills" to good use.

But if you *are* a white supremacist, let me save you some time: you're gonna lose. You always have. Take the Civil War—all those people died, and you lost. The civil rights movement? You lost. And fifty years later, you had a black president. So all the hanging and shooting and violence just delayed the next loss for you. Let's save you some time and declare your loss now. White supremacy is a losing proposition because progress doesn't yield. Literally, you went from blowing up a black church to having a black friend in your lifetime. So, you lost.

JESUS, WHITE PEOPLE'S FAVORITE POC

And it's funny how white nationalists love quoting the Bible, because there are no white people in the Bible. None, not any white person. Jesus never saw a white person.

Y'all know Jesus wasn't white, right? We don't have any Polaroids of him, but he was a Palestinian Jewish man living in the first century, so he didn't have blue eyes and blond hair. Forensic anthropologists have reconstructed what he probably looked like based on skulls of people who lived in the same area at the same time, and they found that he most likely had dark olive skin and short, curly black or brown hair.

So Jesus looked a lot more like *me* than like Brad Pitt in

Legends of the Fall. But the white Jesus is the only one you ever see. That's not Jesus, that's Tristan. Sure, it'd be great if Jesus could kill sinners off with his bowie knife, but I don't know if he needs that.

I mean, we can't know for sure. The only thing that made me think Jesus could be white was that he did turn over all those tables in the temple and didn't go to jail. But I know he was black because he got convicted and killed for a crime he never committed. And he went around with twelve dudes with him all the time.

"Christian values" have caused a lot of pain in the world. You see, I have a problem with the church because the very same people who came up with "nigger" also want to tell us about Jesus. At the same time that they didn't actually believe we had a soul, they taught us about their Lord and Savior. I haven't seen God in a lot of places that niggas are. And Jesus: I find it ironic that the Bible says that we were all created in God's image, but white people had to create him in theirs.

The Jesus that white people worship is amazing. He may not come when you want him to, but he's always on call. Our Jesus takes a lot of weekends off. Maybe, like the cops, Jesus responds quicker to white folks.

I think that's wrong. White people co-opted Jesus in

their image, so when black people pray for salvation, they're asking for help from a white dude. That doesn't usually go so great. I think we gotta make Jesus look like he used to, like 50 Cent in "In Da Club."

Reparations Article 4b. Jesus in Da Club

To restore historical accuracy to the Jesus beloved by white nationalists and black folk alike, and to hopefully make Jesus a bit more accountable to everyone, regardless of the color of their skin, blond-haired, blue-eyed Jesuses shall henceforth be replaced with black Jesuses, modeled after 50 Cent. Jesus will still have abs, just black abs. Also, when there's a manger scene: let's get some black sheep up in that shit too.

WE SHALL BE UN-OPPRESSED

In America, we are still oppressed. In housing and wealth we are left behind. In health, we suffer. The South is still a big fucking problem. In justice and policing, we are discriminated against and abused. This oppression must be countered and lifted!

WE DON'T GET THE SAME EDUCATION AS YOU

Take education: There's never been an honest effort to educate black folks. Never. When the South Carolina Legislature funded the first public school system, they did it because they knew that education is a way out of poverty.

But we don't go to school in the same America as white folks.

FUND OUR SCHOOLS

Local control of schools means that there are huge discrepancies in school funding in different places. Small, rich towns can fund their small, rich—mostly white—schools. Big, poor cities have to make do with less.

On average, nonwhite school districts receive only $11,682 per student each year, compared to $13,908 in predominantly white school districts. Nationwide, that's $23 billion less than white districts for the same number of students. Due to segregation, historic inequities are built into school district borders and the way those school districts are funded.

You can tell a bad school from the name. If you're going to a school named after the KKK founder Nathan Bedford Forrest, I don't have to tell you that it's a shitty school. The way it's funded makes it seem like the KKK is running it. Can you imagine being somebody who hated black people and now the school named after you is full of them? I'm trying to stop your ancestors from rolling over in their graves.

YOU'RE CHEATERS

So let's say that despite the lack of funding, we rise above our shitty schools. Then what? White people always tell us to work hard, get good grades, and then we can go to a good college and get a good job, just like them. And that's true. But it's not the only way.

Let's say that you're a shitty student, but your dad has a lot of money. And let's say your name is Jared Kushner. Then, if your dad donates $2.5 million to Harvard University, it might not be a coincidence when you get in. Big donors get special privileges. People like Les Wexner, the billionaire in charge of Victoria's Secret, donated millions of dollars to Harvard and got three kids in.

But even if you don't have millions of dollars to throw at Harvard, you can still get lucky as long as you're white and your great-grandpappy went to school there in 1789 or whatever.

Take Brett Kavanaugh. According to him, he got into Yale fair and square: "Senator, I was at the top of my class academically, busted my butt in school. Captain of the varsity basketball team. Got in Yale College. When I got into Yale College, got into Yale Law School. Worked my tail off." All that hard work, and still no mention that his grandfather, Everett Edward Kavanaugh, also went to Yale. That's privilege for you: it's all hard work, nothing to do with family connections, it's all a meritocracy—except it isn't.

So a white dude who gets drunk and is accused of sexual assault by multiple women can still become a Supreme Court judge. A black guy who gets a parking ticket and works his way through junior college, goes to law school, what he gets is a TV show about judges. He's Judge Kevin Ross. Judge Kevin Ross is actually a friend of mine. He's like one of the brightest dudes ever. He went to Morehouse, became a judge in Inglewood, and then went on to the California Superior Court. Now he's had a TV show about being a judge for ten years. That's the best we're gonna get.

That's fine, but there's still a difference: Supreme Court or *America's Court*. Judge Kevin Ross might make money, but nobody gives a shit about his opinions. It's all "Pay this bitch her five hundred dollars and let's go home. We ain't got time for this." The difference in the kind of cases you hear is stark: *Citizens United* or *Kayla didn't pay the electric bill.* Come on, man.

And legacy college admissions naturally accrue benefits to white folks whose families were able to attend schools that we weren't allowed in. It's another way that black people get shut out for having the wrong ancestors. Being a legacy can increase your chances of admission by about 20 percent. That's a huge advantage.

I always wanted one of my children to go to the University of Southern California. So I was so happy when my daughter called and she said, "I got accepted to USC." I was on the radio and I started crying. I was able to save the money, my daughter worked hard, played by the rules, and here she is going to the school I always dreamed of. I wish I knew that all I had to do was bribe a motherfucker to say she was on the rowing team. Who knew it was that easy? In March of 2019, the feds busted a bunch of rich parents who shelled out a lot of money to get their kids into schools like USC. For $1.2 million, a girl got into Yale for soccer even though she didn't play soccer. With a lot of cash and a little Photoshop, a girl got admitted to USC as a water polo player. Just put her face on someone else's body and make sure the cash is on the way.

Lori Loughlin and Felicity Huffman paid money to get their kids into schools where slots could have gone to other, more deserving kids. Olivia Jade Giannulli, daughter of Loughlin and fashion designer Mossimo Giannulli, was literally floating around on a yacht when her parents got busted. That yacht, which happened to be owned by Rick Caruso, the elected chair of USC's board of trustees, was probably as close to being on the rowing team as she got.

Now, when you get busted on a yacht for pretending to be on the rowing team—that's some privilege. And Felicity Huffman only served fourteen days in prison for paying to have her daughter's SAT scores fixed. Her lawyers argued that it was her first offense, though the judge neglected to consider her part in *Christmas with the Kranks,* which was an offense to cinema. That shit is the *real* war on Christmas.

Fifteen thousand dollars for good SAT scores and she got fourteen days in jail. You know that has everything to do with her being a rich white lady, because we just gotta look at Tanya McDowell to see that shit is different when you're poor and black. Tanya got charged with "stealing education" because she lied about her address while homeless so her kid could go to a good elementary school. And she was sentenced to prison for five years. Not five days. Five *years*.

At the time there were at least two dozen other families who were found to be violating the residency rules in the district where Tanya enrolled her kid. But because she also had pending drug charges, the authorities threw the book at her. It's fucked up.

So okay, you might not be able to stop rich people from bribing their way into good schools. But even if you don't *bribe* the water polo coach to get your kid into USC, a lot of these sports are just rich-white-kid affirmative action. They're another bit of reverse reparations where black basketball players and football players subsidize sports teams that are full of rich white kids.

Sailing. Water polo. Rowing. What do these sports have in common? They're all white-people sports for kids named Chet, Mitt, or Travis. I mean, with our history, you really want to put a bunch of niggas in a boat and yell at them to row?

And even though nobody's going to the women's water polo matches, somebody's gotta fill that team. So coaches are able to stack these slots on these sports teams with people who wouldn't otherwise get into these schools.

Bribes or no, unpaid black athletes on the money-making football and basketball teams are supporting the admission of white water polo players. We got a problem when Trevon's paying for Tucker. You know what I mean? Kids who grew up shooting hoops are supporting kids who grew up sailing sloops.

And if white people want to pretend that water polo and sailing are real sports, they have to commit to it. I think that every white season-ticket holder for an NCAA basket-ball or football team should also have to be a season-ticket holder for the water polo team. You can't get in to see the Crimson Tide if you haven't been in to see the sailors go out on high tide.

> ### Reparations Article 5a. Sailing Season-Ticket Holders
>
> All supporters of sports of dubious import, the sole purpose of which is admitting their children into college, shall be subject to season-pass requirements. Archery, rowing, fencing, jousting, dressage, or any other stupid sport shall be canceled if there are not enough white parents in attendance at the matches. In addition, every white season-ticket holder for an NCAA basketball or football team shall also be a season-ticket holder for the water polo team.

NO ONE LIKES BAD SPORTS

And while white athletes are playing tennis, black athletes are playing the sports that actually fund the colleges.

So even before this treaty, some people have been thinking about how fair a bargain black athletes are involved in. Are athletes being treated with respect and compensation commensurate with what they bring to universities?

Chris Broussard and Jemele Hill are among the sportswriters thinking about this, calling on minority athletes to "fight power with power" and start going to historically black colleges. Black athletes bring both money and recognition to their schools, so why not keep it in the fam?

Jemele Hill's argument was this: Why do we know about the University of Texas? Why do we know Alabama? Because of their football. All these black kids, these exceptional five-star athletes, go to schools like Texas or Alabama. For years and years, before *Brown v. Board of Education,* black athletes had to go to black schools because they couldn't go anywhere else. But now, the best athletes go to mainstream, majority-white schools.

So when these athletes go to predominantly white schools, they bring resources with them. The athletic programs at Michigan, Ohio State, and Notre Dame pay a ton of bills. Twenty-seven schools make at least $100 million a year from their athletic departments. Michigan State makes $54 million in licensing, $59 million from football, and $18 million from basketball. Look at all the money generated from athletes: from parking to concessions to merchandising. So if you're Magic Johnson, you go to Michigan State and all those boosters come to see you play in those games and you pay for a lot of shit just running that ball. Imagine if those same monies were in black schools. The buildings would be better. The professors would be better. The facilities would be better.

And these schools really are white schools, run on black athletes' money. Black men are only a tiny percent of the student population, but they're the majority of the athletes. Without that money, these schools' teams would be nothing. Jemele Hill argued in an *Atlantic* article that a concerted movement back to historically black colleges and universities (HBCUs) would benefit the places that have the greatest impact on the black professional class in America: "Despite constituting only 3 percent of four-year colleges in the country, HBCUs have produced 80 percent of the black judges, 50 percent of the black lawyers, 50 percent of the black doctors, 40 percent of the black engineers, 40 percent of the black members of Congress, and 13 percent of the black CEOs in America today."

These games are giant advertisements for the schools. A lot of white people know about USC only because it's got great basketball and football traditions. I don't care how many Pulitzer Prize or Nobel Prize winners come out of your school; you don't get no commercials on Saturdays. Black athletes are bringing in that money.

And you know what else? Everybody loves niggas on a Sunday, because that's when the football games are on. And most people's sports heroes are black. If that's where we gotta start—if that's what gets some white people to respect or admire a black person—I don't want to take that one day away from them. You know what I mean? Let's build from there. Pretty soon we got people liking us Sunday through Wednesday, at least.

So here's the deal: We want a fair share of the revenue coming in for our efforts. And we want funding for our HBCUs, which, after all, benefit everyone. With all the problems in education, you want to be sure there are places educating black people effectively. The endowments of these schools are far below those of Ivy League schools, but their impact on diversity in the professional class is huge.

And in return, we'll play ball. If you have a college sports program, you need black people in it if you want people to watch it. When people sit out in the snow with paint on their faces, they don't want to see some bullshit. If black people didn't play football, it would be rugby. You don't want that. The only time you watch rugby is when you lose your fucking remote.

Reparations Article 5b. Pay Up, or Rugby

The sport of rugby, being abhorrent in nature, undesirable to both black and white, who do both enjoy the Sundays spent watching "the Big Game," shall henceforth be set aside in favor of keeping black athletes playing ball. Black athletes will play ball if white supporters will likewise play ball, financing historically black colleges and universities, paying athletes their worth, and generally respecting the fact that nobody would give a fuck about Alabama without Tua Tagovailoa.

WE CAN'T LIVE WHERE WE WANT TO

The oppression continues in education, housing, and banking to this day. We still can't live where we want to, and we still don't share in America's wealth.

WHERE THE BLACK PEOPLE AREN'T

A few years ago, Jon Stewart tried to call Bill O'Reilly on his white privilege. O'Reilly, of course, wants to deny that such a thing exists and wants to pretend that he's some kind of Johnny Lunchpail, a self-made man from a tough working-class background who pulled himself up by his bootstraps. Bill O'Reilly talks in his book *The O'Reilly Factor* about growing up in Levittown, Long Island, the iconic post–World War II suburban development. Levittown was built as one of the first suburban communities for returning GIs, who could pick up a house for $7,990 with TV included. Using a GI loan, you paid 0 percent interest. Well, you know what my father couldn't get? A GI loan.

That's because the GI Bill was deliberately structured to shut black veterans out. The chair of the House's committee on veterans, Mississippi congressman John Rankin, made sure that it was administered by states, not the federal government, thus making sure that racist state governments would have control of it. Rankin was a capital-*R* racist, on the record for saying civil rights would destroy "the white man's civilization throughout the world." Jim Crow was alive and well at the time, and Rankin thought that warm feelings for returning GIs would generate gains for blacks that he couldn't tolerate.

The local administration of the bill denied opportunities to black veterans. Racist policies of the states ensured that loans were given out to whites, not blacks. Many white-run banks refused mortgages and loans to black people, even though the VA would cosign the loan. So even after fighting a war, black veterans were shut out of the honor they deserved. According to the Equal Justice Initiative, "A survey of 13 Mississippi cities found that African Americans received only 2 of the 3229 home, business, and farm loans administered by the VA in 1947." This didn't just happen in the South; in New York and New Jersey, fewer than 100 of the 67,000 mortgages insured by the GI Bill were for black people's homes. Yet black people's taxes financed that shit for you too. We paid taxes but didn't get shit.

But even if my dad had the money, he wouldn't have been allowed to buy the same house as Bill O'Reilly's dad's. At Levittown, no niggers were allowed. It was written right into the original charter that no "non-Caucasians" could own or rent in Levittown. Eventually, that got struck down in court, but discrimination continued and even today the suburb is 94 percent white. Charters like this were widespread. The executive producer for my show dug up the old charter for his neighborhood and it says you can't sell to black people. That's two miles from where I work right now.

So the GI Bill was designed for white people and Levittown was designed for white people.

And this isn't ancient history—the same thing is still happening today. *Newsday* just did a three-year investigation of the real estate industry on Long Island and found that black people are still being discriminated against, steered away from white neighborhoods and into black neighborhoods.

One real estate agent told a white buyer to stay away from a mostly minority neighborhood because of gang violence but didn't discourage a black buyer who had the same budget. Agents sent white buyers to Merrick, a white area. And when talking to a black buyer about Brentwood, a black and Hispanic area where there's MS-13 gang violence, an agent said that residents there were the "nicest people."

The undercover investigation showed that real estate agents treated black people unequally 49 percent of the time, compared to white people. A lot of this treatment was subtle—discrepancies in what houses people were shown or requiring preapproved mortgages before showing listings.

The black buyers would really have no idea that they were being treated differently. But they were given fewer listings and were steered into different areas than white people.

When I was a brand-new young dude, twenty-four or twenty-five, looking to buy a new house, the same thing happened to me in L.A. I specifically said I wanted to move out of the neighborhood and yet they only showed me houses in Compton or in deep L.A. I must have looked at ten houses that day and none of them was four miles away from where I was currently living. It was like: you take a left, then another left, then another left, and we're back where we started. I almost rebought my own house, except my price was too high.

So the discrimination is different, but it's real. It's biased real estate agents. And it's unfair practices.

It's not like people put ads in the paper anymore that say, "Whites Only," but then again, people don't put any ads in papers. It's all online now. In March 2019, the Department of Housing and Urban Development sued Facebook for allowing housing discrimination by way of targeted advertising. It allowed users to target ads excluding people by race, just like in the old days. When *ProPublica* did an investigation of similar practices in 2016, it found that Facebook discriminated based on "ethnic affinity." A spokesman pointed out that ethnic affinity is not the same as race—but I'm gonna guess that when you discriminate against "African American affinity," you're not just targeting Eminem and Vanilla Ice. Turns out that the people with the greatest African American affinity are black people. If that ain't racist, it's at least affinity-ist.

So fine, if you want to keep saying that you come from a hardscrabble town and modest means and built yourself up from nothing, go ahead. Tell everyone you came from Levittown or Steelburg or Old Scranton. We understand how important these old places are to your sense of belonging and to your story.

But if you're going to do that, we want you to make a slight modification, a clarification to your origin story. Please only refer to these towns with the preface "All-White." So if you want to say you came from Levittown or Steelburg, you must now call it "All-White Levittown" or "All-White Steelburg," as in, "Yes, I came from humble beginnings: my dad used to dig for potatoes in the fields of All-White Potatotown," or "It weren't easy for me ma and pa, all day me ma would cook meals and run the PTA and me pa would commute to an accounting firm in the city. At night, we'd all huddle around the dining room table and enjoy a big dinner in the traditional All-White Levittown way."

Reparations Article 5c. Truth in Advertising

White people, being beneficiaries of racist housing policies, having written the rules to ensure all-white suburbs, and having extended opportunity to whites only, shall henceforth retain their cherished lies about the lack of privilege and opportunity that they had. Not having lacked for privilege and opportunity, they shall nonetheless henceforth have the privilege and opportunity of lack: that is, they shall retain the opportunity to say they did not have much, grew up in humble circumstances, are self-made in every way. However, if a place is named in such recollections, if an anecdote of their upbringing is in the offing, they must amend the place-name with the preface "All-White" to bring a bit of truth to the lie.

WE FELL INTO THE GAP

And policies like this have created a wealth gap, even in the modern era. The original homes in Levittown only cost you $7,990, but the median price today is $400,000. That's what building wealth in real estate gets you. And it's what we missed out on.

According to McKinsey & Company,

the median white family had more than ten times the wealth of the median black family in 2016. In fact, the racial wealth gap between black and white families grew from about $100,000 in 1992 to $154,000 in 2016, in part because white families gained significantly more wealth (with the median increasing by $54,000), while median wealth for black families did not grow at all in real terms over that period.

Home ownership is one of the biggest generators of family wealth over time, because you can buy a starter home, it (hopefully) accrues value, and you sell it to buy a bigger home. That's been a part of the American Dream for decades. But it doesn't work for us.

Just being in a black neighborhood costs you money.

The Brookings Institution found that in neighborhoods that are at least 50 percent black, the homes are valued at half the price of homes in nonblack neighborhoods. And it's not because the houses or neighborhoods are worse. According to Brookings, "Homes of similar quality in neighborhoods with similar amenities are worth 23 percent less in majority black neighborhoods, compared to those with very few or no black residents." And even when you adjust for crime rates, commute times, etc., it only explains about half of the undervaluation. On average, having a "black" house costs you $48,000. Across all majority black neighborhoods, that's a $156 billion loss. Let that sink in. That's $156 billion that racial bias pulls from our pockets.

When I was selling my house in West Hills, Los Angeles—a brand-new house—this shit happened to me. We had lived there for three years and my wife wanted to move. So we remodeled the house, and we were getting an appraisal and my real estate broker told us to put our family pictures away during the appraisal. I said, "I'm not taking my fucking pictures down." And I didn't do it.

And the appraisal came in so low that the bank called us and they're like, "Is the property in disrepair?" I mean, this was a new house, only a few years old, and I had put in a pool and hardwood floors and new counters. There were still houses being built on my street. The bank couldn't understand why the appraisal was so low; the comps in the area were much higher. So they talked to the appraiser and asked why it was so low and he said, "Because I just thought it was accurate. Because it is what I say it is."

So he tried to take $160,000 of real value from my home. They fired that appraiser and got another one, and my house ended up selling for the comps. And I was able to take the profit from that and buy another house. I was lucky, luckier than most black people. But damn if it wasn't a wake-up moment.

So you all freed us, but then wouldn't let us live where we wanted. You restricted where we could move, then wouldn't give us loans for the places you let us go. And now, you steer us back to those same places, those same neighborhoods.

When we do have a house, it gets devalued because we live in it. And we get offered worse mortgages. Wells Fargo had to pay $175 million in 2012 because of their predatory lending practices. Researchers found that black borrowers in Baltimore were given loans that cost an average of $15,000 to $16,000 more over the thirty-year term than white borrowers' loans.

All of this has led to where we are now: the lowest black home ownership rates since the 1960s. The Urban Institute showed a huge gap between black and white home ownership: from 2001 to 2016, the black home ownership rate dropped five points to 41 percent, as opposed to a one-point decline for whites to 71 percent.

Then when you need to run a highway somewhere, or build an airport, you take our houses.

EMINENT DOMAIN AND HIGHWAYS

In L.A., there's this freeway, the 105. It goes right through our neighborhoods. The 105 is like a lot of highway projects: The government comes in and takes your house by eminent domain. If you bought a house for thirty grand, they say, "I'll give you thirty-two, now get out."

My wife's grandmother owned a house along the freeway's proposed path, and they took it from her forty or fifty years ago to build the 105. She had bought this home for $15,000, and today a shitty house in that area is $350,000. Just the property is worth that much.

All the time these highways go through poor neighborhoods inhabited by people of color. So even when you have a big chip in the game, the powers that be are able to take it away. Imagine how much wealth you'd have if you had just been able to keep that house and accrue the benefits over time. There are houses now in Inglewood that are worth more than $750,000 that were originally $20,000. They could have changed people's lives.

All of this is made possible even though the Fifth Amendment of the Constitution specifies that the government can't take private property. The exception to this rule is taking property for "public use." But a lot of the time, this "public use" is for "urban renewal," itself a disguised bit of racist code for "take black people's shit."

Because all the highways go through black neighborhoods, I think that black people shouldn't have to pay any tolls. By this agreement, we'll create a new E-ZPass for black folks—let's call it a Take It Easy Pass.

Reparations Article 5d. Take It Easy Pass

Until such a time as highways are put through white neighborhoods, and in consideration of the inequal use of eminent domain, the building of highway projects in black neighborhoods, and the drawbacks that accrue therefrom, black people shall be issued Easy Passes that provide discounted (free) tolls for all highways.

And furthermore, the toll roads need to be adjusted to prioritize black drivers. High-Occupancy Vehicle lanes gotta change. Not HOV, but BOV lanes: Black-Occupancy Vehicles. Of course, we do run a risk putting all the black drivers in one lane, 'cause the cops will know exactly who to pull over. I don't feel like helping the cops that much, so tell you what: In some places, you can pay to use the HOV lane even if you're just driving alone, right? So maybe we can incentivize some white people to use the lane, making a little money on the deal and mitigating the risk of everyone in the lane getting pulled over. Finally, some white people will get pulled over for DWB.

Levittown was built for white people, but there's never been a housing development built for black people. None. Except jail. Even the projects weren't originally built for black people. They were built for people coming back from the armed services. And it's funny that all the places that are the roughest are named after cool shit. It's always "gardens" and "terraces" and "villages." If you heard the names of the places we live; all the projects sound beautiful. Hacienda Village, Cabrini-Green, and Nigger-Free Gardens . . . but the prettier the name, the shittier the neighborhood.

There's never been anywhere that was designed with the

idea of attracting a lot of black people. So even the homes that we have, people didn't want us to have. Compton is called the Hub City because it's in the center of all of L.A. But before World War II, Compton was 95 percent white. By 1970, due to white flight, 65 percent of the population was black. Compton has an airport. They didn't build the airport because they knew niggas was gonna be there. They didn't know Dr. Dre was gonna be there. I mean, Kevin Costner lived in the neighborhood. So everywhere we go, one nigga moved in and white people moved out. There was nowhere we were invited to live.

THE COLOR PURPLE

And black neighborhoods don't have stores that fit our needs. We only get stuff when we leave, and then we aren't there to enjoy it. When we move out, white people move in and bring everything with them. Gentrification is funny because those are the same structures, just new people. Gentrification is black people having enough money to move out and white people having enough money to move in, but they bring Starbucks and grocery stores and opportunity with them. But we don't have that shit. You can go to the Magic Johnson Theatre, but how many times can you watch *Juice* or *Boyz n the Hood*? If you're a black person, you'll never see an independent film in your neighborhood.

I mean, we can live without seeing *The Royal Tenenbaums,* but we can't live without grocery stores. It's seventeen miles on average before black people can access fresh produce or fresh meat. Grocery stores just don't open in our neighborhoods the way that dollar stores and liquor stores do. The Greenwood section of Tulsa, former home of Black Wall Street, went from having dozens of grocery stores to having none. But it does have eight dollar stores. Dollar stores are replacing grocery stores in poor communities of color throughout the country. These sorts of stores have a very limited amount of fresh food, if any.

So we can't get fresh fruit, but we can get Fabuloso. Black people love Fabuloso for some reason. We used to have grocery stores where you could get Pine-Sol or Ajax. But when dollar stores came, they brought the cheapest bullshit, so all you can get is Fabuloso. It's a Spanish name, but we're probably their biggest customer. So now niggas is buying shit they can't pronounce. Fabuloso virtually killed Pine-Sol for niggas. You ain't gonna smell a fresh pine scent in a black neighborhood. Black neighborhoods smell purple.

It wasn't like that ten years ago. I didn't used to know

what Fabuloso was. My housekeeper brought it into my house, and I was like, "What the fuck is Fabuloso?" But then all of a sudden, every black person's house that I'd go over to would have Fabuloso. All because of dollar stores. Dollar stores have become our corner store, our hardware store, our grocery store.

And who knows what the hell is in Fabuloso? Nature don't make shit that purple, so you know it ain't plant based. According to its website, it's got sodium dodecyl-benzenesulfonate in it. Sodium dodecylbenzenesulfonate? That looks like a Word Jumble, not an ingredient. You're not gonna find that shit at Whole Foods or Trader Joe's. They don't make organic sodium dodecylbenzenesulfonate. So one of the things that happens to us is we use things that are not environmentally safe. And we only have access to food that's bad for us. And then, who becomes the burden on society? Meanwhile, all these people getting rich off of folks who they made sick are like, "You're on your own." It's a weird nexus.

Black and brown neighborhoods are more likely to have hazardous compounds in the air. The highways that cut through and surround poor neighborhoods cause nitrogen oxides from exhaust fumes. Air pollution from industrial sites, truck routes, and ports contributes to higher asthma rates and other poor health outcomes. According to a Yale University study, black people had a higher exposure than white people for thirteen out of fourteen pollutants.

So black people get more:

- Air pollution
- Lead
- Asthma
- Dollar stores
- Fast food
- Fabuloso

And we get less:

- Nature
- Grocery stores
- Art-house cinemas
- Fresh food
- Pine-Sol

So what do we want? We want fair access to the shit you all got. We want facilities: grocery stores, movie theaters, and better food.

Reparations Article 5e. Near Our Houses: Actual Food

We need actual food in our neighborhoods: quality grocery stores with fresh fruit, vegetables, and meats. For the purposes of this agreement, neither a pile of bananas by the cash register nor any meat in a can shall constitute "fresh," regardless of the packaging's claims. We want real restaurants and coffee shops; the McCafé section of a McDonald's shall not count. We want environmental justice, so that we don't have to use Fabuloso to scrub out the pollutants in our homes. We want that fresh pine smell and that fresh clean air you all got.

And now it's moving in reverse. African Americans are moving to the outlying areas. They're not living in the cities no more, because cities are becoming untenable for us. And we're not moving to the good suburbs; we're moving to places far away and shitty. Like San Bernardino is suburban, but it's all niggas and it's horrible. So they just moved the projects to San Bernardino and moved all the bullshit with them. All you did was change the background on *Cops*.

But we live where we can. The only reason we're in the

hoods is because we have to be there. My parents *had* to live where they lived; they were not allowed to live anywhere else. Most black people lived where we were forced to live. Between being told that you can't have a house here and facing charters against selling to black people or banks refusing to lend, the places that we live in are the places we had to live in.

In the '70s, people thought there was a CIA plot to cordon black people into concentration camps: the King Alfred Plan. The King Alfred Plan came from a novel, *The Man Who Cried I Am* by John A. Williams, and was invented as part of his publicity campaign for the book. He left copies of these "secret" plans on subway cars and they spread to activist communities, who were unsure whether the plans were real or not. So it's fictional, but we actually *do* live in areas cordoned off by the government. King Alfred is nothing like Fat Albert, and maybe both are fictional, but they represent something real. Some people call it redlining, some people call it camps. But the bottom line is you can't get loans there. And you're only shown certain houses. And you can only get approved to live in certain places. So how is that demonstrably different from a "fictitious CIA-led plot"? Who needs the CIA? You have Coldwell Banker or Bank of America.

WE'RE NOT AS HEALTHY AS YOU

And when you have to live in a bad neighborhood, when you don't have money or access to good food and resources, you're not as healthy.

GET THE LEAD OUT

The only person who still uses lead pipes is Mrs. Peacock, in the conservatory. It was either her or Colonel Mustard in the billiard room with the rope. But I digress.

Well, also black people and other people of color in Flint. Oh, and in Newark. And Pittsburgh, Baltimore, and who knows where else.

Everybody knows that lead is dangerous. Lead exposure has been linked to increases in crime, lower IQs, and behavioral disorders. If you look at most people in prison, they have a couple of things in common: they're illiterate and they have high concentrations of lead in their blood.

The fall in violent crime beginning in the 1990s wasn't due to "broken windows" policing or "zero tolerance" policies. It wasn't stop-and-frisk. It was a drop in people's lead levels. Higher childhood blood lead levels are associated with higher adult arrest rates for violent crimes. The drop in crime corresponds with the banning of leaded gasoline emissions that caused the majority of lead exposure in children.

The impact on black urban populations can't be over-stated. Your environment has an impact on you physiolog-ically and physically, but it's easier to blame illiteracy and crime on "cultural" problems than on environmental fac-tors. The black culture is violent, prisons have to be built, and so on.

But let's not get off track. So you say there's a cultural problem, we say there's a lead problem. Tell you what: let's at least take care of one of the problems that we all agree on—nobody thinks lead is a good idea anymore. It's out of gas, but there's still a lot of old lead paint and a lot of old lead pipes.

In Flint, in Newark, and elsewhere they keep fucking things up by trying to add chemicals to the water and then send everyone a bunch of filters and water bottles when it doesn't work. Well, enough. We want new pipes. No more lead pipes, no more bottled water deliveries. I don't care if it's Fiji or Poland Spring, it's got to go.

And we need a big paint job, a Sherwin-Williams' March to remove lead paint from our homes. Y'all love home reno-vation shows: Think of this like one big HGTV project. The flips have flopped—now we need Chip and Joanna Gaines to come out and fix shit up. You won't find a bigger fixer-upper than the neighborhoods that still have lead paint.

Reparations Article 5f. Black Neighborhood Rehab

It's makeover time for black neighborhoods, due to the lead pipes and paint. We hereby demand that the HGTV network send some of their experts in to get the lead out and spruce the place up, preferably that Chip and Joanna couple, as long as Chip keeps the corny jokes to a minimum. If they are busy, we'll take the Property Brothers.

This treaty might be a bitter pill, so I want to throw you a few easy wins: things that you can agree to that will take the sting out. Some of this shit will even *save* you money, instead of costing you money. Kevin Drum of *Mother Jones* estimates that cleaning up lead could cost about $20 billion a year but would still save us all money in higher IQs, higher incomes, and drops in crime to the tune of about $200 billion a year. Doing something that everyone agrees is a good idea *and* saving money? Yep.

You don't want another white governor getting blamed for another lead pipe problem. You don't want another "the next Flint." Trust me: there's not a big enough Brita filter to take care of this shit.

KEEP MEDICAL RACISM

I've spent a lot of this book criticizing racism, but I don't want to seem totally negative about it; I mean, maybe some good has come of it after all.

For example, because of racism, we didn't get hooked on opiates like white folks did. Doctors, traditionally, don't believe black people feel as much pain, so they prescribe them less medication. Multiple studies have shown this to be the case. When black patients complain of pain similar to that of white patients, they are less likely to be given pain meds, and if they are, it's at a lower dosage than whites.

Some part of this is probably overprescription of medication to white people, of course. But part of it has been shown to be due to bias and misguided beliefs about biological differences between the races, including beliefs that black people are stronger and feel less pain than whites. The only time I feel no pain is when I've had a little too much Rémy Martin. I mean, when a doctor says, "You know, I hate niggers," it's not good. But because he hated niggas, I didn't OD in a bathroom. So, you know—in this one way it kinda worked out for us. Because of institutional biases and racism, we missed that whole scene.

Doctors have never believed black people can feel pain. In a way, it's put black people at the forefront of many medical breakthroughs, although maybe not in the way you'd usually like. For instance, take the experiments of the "father of modern gynecology," J. Marion Sims, who relied on the contributions of black women to perfect surgical techniques. His achievement was marked, until recently, with a statue of Sims in Central Park across from the New York Academy of Medicine. I probably don't have to tell you that someone called the "father of modern gynecology" has turned out to have a problematic past. Did you see that coming? Well, unfortunately, these surgical techniques were perfected on enslaved black women without anesthesia. His statue was pulled recently because, as the New York City Public Design Commission said, "Free consent to participate in the experiments was not obtainable from women who were not free." *Another fucking statue we had to deal with!*

So yeah, we were at the forefront of medical discovery, but as test *subjects*.

And it's not just experiments like this and the Tuskegee syphilis experiments that make black people distrust doctors. There's something about white guys in white robes that makes us nervous, you know?

Black people don't have a high trust of doctors for good reason. Take Serena Williams: she nearly died after childbirth because doctors didn't believe she had a blood clot. The day after her C-section, she felt short of breath. Because she's a badass, she was able to advocate for herself and alert the medical staff. She walked out of her hospital room and told the nurses that she needed "a CT scan with contrast and IV heparin right away." How many people would know to order that shit? When they did the scan, it showed small blood clots in her lungs that could have killed her.

Medical bias is a real thing. The Centers for Disease Control and Prevention reported that black women were three times more likely than white women to suffer a pregnancy-related death. Serena's experience isn't uncommon for black women; a lot of these deaths happen the day after delivery, or even several weeks later.

When medical care is less available and doctors exhibit bias, the outcomes are worse. Black women are more likely to go into pregnancy with underlying health problems because they don't have as much health care access. And it's not just because of less insurance coverage; studies have shown that mothers avoid prenatal care when they feel like they face bias and bad treatment from medical staff.

Black women and white women get breast cancer at about the same rate, but black women die from it at a higher rate than white women, as an example. Why? They've only recently tried to figure it out. The institutional bias in the medical industry is to study white people and not black people. Only recently, after other studies included mostly white women, did a Black Women's Health Study get launched out of Boston University to specifically study the health of fifty-nine thousand black women. This study figured out that black women are more likely to develop the most aggressive form of breast cancer. And it turns out that being born in a Southern state that used to have Jim Crow laws raised black women's risk of being diagnosed with breast tumors. Racism kills.

But again, I don't want to sound like the lack of medical care and institutional biases of the Southern states are all bad.

Let me thank the Republican Party, especially Republican governors who fought so hard against expanding Obamacare. Because if you don't have health insurance, you're not getting opiates. Lack of health coverage has been a huge help here. And you'll never guess who's lagging behind in health coverage. Just prior to the launch of Obamacare, black people had a much higher uninsured rate than white people, and since its passage that gap has narrowed a bit. But in states where Republicans blocked the Medicaid expansion, that uninsured rate is still nearly twice as high as in states that passed the Medicaid expansion. That's basically the South and parts of the Midwest, ya know, where most black people live.

Have you ever noticed that only rich niggas OD on opiates? That's why. Nobody can afford the coverage it takes to get hooked on opiates. I mean, $2,500 a month with a $500 copay? You need money to get hooked like that. Prince? Come on, now. Prince died because he started taking pain meds for hip pain. If only people had been more racist toward Prince, he might have lived. You know, if you can die the same way as Tom Petty, you're dying like a white guy.

Reparations Article 5g. Stay Racist, Medically

White people, unable to eliminate racism and bias in all forms, are hereby allowed to remain racist in matters of prescribing medicine, especially opioids and pain medications. With expanded access to health care, we understand that risks to us increase, but we'll worry about that when y'all approve Obamacare's Medicaid expansion anywhere in the South at all. In the meantime, if a wealthy black person requires pain meds, please remember that he "Got the Look" of a black dude, so he ain't "Free Fallin'" into a coma.

THE SOUTH MUST SURRENDER PROPERLY

You know, it seems like I've spent a lot of the book criticizing the South. Well, the South has a lot of problems for black people. And if the white people in the South had surrendered properly the first time around, we might not even need this treaty.

YOU LIVE FOR LESS IN THE SOUTH

The largest percentage of black people in America live in the South. You can live for less in the South. But the *chance* to live is lower.

It doesn't cost you money, it costs you years. In California, your life expectancy is 81 years. But if you live in Mississippi, it's 74.5 years. That's less than the life expectancy in

Bulgaria or Malaysia. The average life expectancy in America is 78.6 years. But all across the South, you'll live less than that on average: North Carolina, Georgia, South Carolina, Tennessee, Louisiana, Kentucky, Alabama, West Virginia, and Mississippi.

Black people who live in more diverse areas live longer, make more money, and are better educated. When the Associated Press looked at county-level data of life expectancy, they found that a lot of the same issues that plague the black population generally are also correlated with life expectancy. Life expectancy increased with an increase in median income and decreased with increases in unemployment or lower education levels. It decreased by eight months with a 10 percent increase in the black population. Of the areas with the lowest life expectancy, about half are majority-black populations, 51 percent have low education, and 61 percent have low incomes. Most of the places where people die the earliest are black places.

MEET THE FLINTSTONES

It's like America's made up of the Flintstones and the Jetsons, and the Flintstones are running the country. They want to stop cars with their feet instead of jetting around. You think the Green New Deal is a stupid idea, but coal mining's smart? Come again? You like working for Mr. Slate when you could be working for Cosmo Spacely? They're so backward, they want to deport Rosie the Robot.

Who benefited more from the Civil War: black people or white people in the South? Even the losers of that war benefited more than the people who the war was fought over. And these states are still run by white legislatures and governors.

The South is still a mess for black people. Fifty-four percent of African Americans live in the Southern region of the United States, but somehow, it's still run by white people. Eighteen percent of black folks live in the Northeast, 19 percent live in the Midwest, and 10 percent live in the West. Republicans are in charge all across the South, even though more black people are concentrated in the South than in all the other regions combined. And for some reason, this region is primarily the poorest, the most in need of government assistance. If white people are so smart, why can't they get their shit together in the South? Maybe if the white governments of these states worked a little harder on making things good for their constituents instead of trying to knock black people down, they'd get more done.

The South has been set up to take away freedoms from black people. India's constitution is 177,000 words and they've got billions of people. The U.S. Constitution is 4,543 words with 27 amendments. The Alabama State Constitution has more than 300,000 words and 892 amendments. The United States learned a long time ago that taking freedoms away is problematic. They tried to do Prohibition and it was repealed. Most of the amendments have given people more rights, not less. Alabama's constitution is all about restrictions. When it was written, it was specifically designed to retain white supremacy in the state, including sections against interracial marriage and maintaining the segregation of public schools. I really don't understand how you have 300,000 words and you're fiftieth in education. All them words and you still can't read? You cut out the words "no" and "hate" and you're down to 150,000 words, easy.

The South is still about oppressing black people. Have you ever noticed that all of these states where they frown more on doctors who perform abortions than they do people who commit rape and incest are the same states where it was okay to rape slaves? A woman's body wasn't ever really her own. I wonder how many white people in the South would be for abortion when they find out they're going to have a black grandbaby.

And Mississippi only officially outlawed slavery in 2013.

Mississippi was one of the only states to not ratify the Thir-teenth Amendment banning slavery. When three-fourths of the states ratified the amendment in 1865, it became law. Every other state ratified the amendment, but Mississippi didn't. It was only after a Mississippi resident saw the movie *Lincoln* and did a little research that he realized that even though Mississippi had voted to ratify the amendment in 1995, it had failed to make it official by notifying the U.S. archivist. They were like, "Hey, fellas, we'll be right back. There's something we forgot to do." And so they finally ratified it 148 years late.

That's how backwards shit is. Just last year, they found the last slave ship to reach the United States in Mobile, Alabama. Researchers found the remains of the *Clotilda,* the boat that carried 110 slaves to Alabama in 1860, in the mud of the Mobile River. And the crazy thing is that it was still working. They had to tell the skipper to get off. "Why? I got deliveries to make."

In parts of the South, people are still trying to defend the "traditional" Southern way of life. "Tradition" is a great way to keep stuff the same as it always was—i.e., racist. Segre-gation has been outlawed in the United States, but in some places in the South, racially segregated proms have been a "tradition" that's only recently been challenged. Mississippi fully integrated its schools in 1970, but some places still had "black proms" and "white proms." In 1997, Morgan Freeman offered to pay for a racially mixed prom in his hometown of Charleston, Mississippi, but it took until 2008 for it to happen. The same is true in places like Rochelle, Georgia, which had its first mixed prom in 2014.

The reason for these separate proms? "Tradition." So when do you decide to get rid of "traditions" like this? When do we get the full rights of American citizens?

Virtually every city that black people are doing well in is either in a blue state or the blue city of a red state. I think it's gonna stay that way. Even when it seems like a black politician is going to take charge, the old racist voter suppression machine kicks into high gear. If not for voter suppression, we'd have at least two black governors in the South: Stacey Abrams in Georgia and Andrew Gillum in Florida. In Georgia, Abrams's opponent was the secretary of state overseeing the election, a clear conflict of interest. He purged 670,000 voter registrations in the year before the election and another 53,000 right before. And in Florida, Gillum lost by fewer than 30,000 votes after a recount and a campaign where his opponent, Ron DeSantis, urged people not to "monkey up" the election by electing Gillum.

It's always hilarious to me how all these MAGA-hat-wearing red-state Republicans are always complaining about taxes, about "makers and takers," and about "draining the swamp," when they're the ones *getting* the tax money, *they're* the takers, and the swamp benefits them more than anybody.

Mississippi, Kentucky, West Virginia, Alabama, and South Carolina are all in the top ten states that depend the most on federal funds to support their government and residents. As far as "makers" go, Alabama, West Virginia, Arkansas, and Mississippi all have the lowest gross domestic product of the states, and yet Mississippi and West Virginia still get the highest amount of money in federal grants—pretty swampy!

I think America would be better off if we moved most of the black folks out of the South and let white people have it. Sell this shit back to white people and get a credit on our statement. We'll give you a discount and move some of you white folks from California and other nice spots to the South, your treasured homeland. We're handing it back to you, gently used. This land is your land, this land is made for you and you.

Reparations Article 5h. Reverse Louisiana Purchase

White people, having worked very hard to retain the South during the Civil War and having used voter suppression and other tactics to retain power, shall be given the South—just not all the good parts—to do with as they wish. No federal funds (handouts) nor voting powers beyond local control shall be retained, to make sure that the South can credibly claim the right to say they are self-sufficient. Let them build pride in their work, allow them the dignity of work.

In the South we'll establish a territory for white people. It might be a little swampy, a little humid, and I can't guarantee that you won't have problems with global warming. Let's hope your conservative leaders are right about it being a hoax.

Now, you might have some reservations about this plan, but hear me out. Excuse my choice of words. Come to think of it, that's a good name for this territory: a reservation. This'll give you the opportunity to help you prove your theories about states' rights and the value of local control. We won't be sending you federal dollars, because we know you hate handouts. This time we'll let you out of the Union with our blessing, without our free labor. Let's see if you can be self-sufficient. Will the South rise again? I'll wait and see.

FREEDOM, BUT NOT FREE

It's a shame that the most underused, the most undervalued part of the word "freedom" is "free."

Now that we've got the Southern states squared away, let's talk about the state of justice in America. Slavery is over, but we've basically gone from slavery to prisons. There's still no justice for us.

FREE LABOR

See, black people get a little sensitive about "free labor." When your ancestors were enslaved and then forced into labor under vagrancy laws, you tend to be *touchy* about being forced to work.

So during the 2019 government shutdown, predictably it was a white congressman who said, "Never in the history of this country has it been legal to make people work for free but that's what's happening to federal employees." Um, *there was this one time*.

Slavery was just swapped for the judicial system. Like

John Legend pointed out in his Oscar speech in 2015: "We live in the most incarcerated country in the world. There are more black men under correctional control today than there were under slavery in 1850." After slavery ended, black men were targeted by their former masters, arrested for vagrancy, loitering, and other concocted offenses. Once in custody, they were leased as laborers to farms and businesses. How wrong is that? But it ain't over. It's still happening.

Prisoners are used as cheap or free labor, making less than a dollar an hour to do work for corporations and the government. Major corporations like Victoria's Secret and Starbucks have used that labor. Hundreds of thousands of prisoners work making furniture, in call centers—even fighting fires.

Originally this prison labor was supposed to be rehabilitative—you learn a skill that you can apply when you get on the outside. Like a shittier DeVry. But a lot of these jobs aren't available to inmates after they leave. In California, prisoners are fighting wildfires for between $2.90 and $5.12 a day, putting their lives at risk. But when they come out after they got real-life experience, guess who they don't get to be? Firefighters.

Free black labor is part of an economic model. There's no incentive to stop it. People don't usually come out and say it like that, but sometimes they let an "oopsie" loose, like when the sheriff of Louisiana's Caddo Parish criticized a prison reform bill by saying, "They're releasing some good ones that we use every day to wash cars, to change oil in the cars, to cook in the kitchen, to do all that where we save money." So you're keeping people in jail because you need people to wash your cars or cook in your kitchen? What would you do without the prisoners? I don't know. Hire people?

Can't hire people? Listen, I'm not against interns. Maybe work for college credit or something.

And it's not enough that your labor's being exploited; in forty-nine states, they also bill you for prison. In Florida, they can charge you fifty dollars a day, payable upon your release. After one former inmate, Jeremy Barrett, was assaulted in prison, he sued the Florida Department of Corrections for negligence, only to get a counterclaim of $54,750. In some parts of the country, you can be charged all sorts of fees: for incarceration, DNA tests, use of a public defender, court costs, and more. It's to always keep you chained to the system.

HIGH CRIMES

A lot of black men are in prison just for selling weed. And we know now that this is a failed policy because eleven states and D.C. have already legalized it. Between 2001 and 2010, there were 8.2 million arrests for marijuana. And even though blacks and whites use weed at about the same rate, blacks are four times more likely to be arrested for it. All of these useless arrests and all of these wasted lives.

And while black dudes are in prison, white dudes like Kevin Murphy, the CEO of the marijuana company Acreage Holdings, get rich. In the first quarter of 2019, Acreage reported revenue of $12.9 million. From Kevin Murphy's bio:

> Prior to his role at Acreage Holdings, Kevin was most recently a Founding Member and Managing Partner of Tandem Global Partners, a boutique investment firm focused on the emerging markets. Previously, he was Managing Partner at Stanfield Capital Partners, where he served as a member of the Operating and Management team that oversaw all aspects of Stanfield's business, including risk management, sales and distribution, client services, legal, compliance and operations.

You know, he learned his trade on the mean streets of Tandem Global Partners. Normally, when a drug dealer talks about "risk management" and "sales and distribution," they're being euphemistic for taking out their enemies and slinging dope—but this guy really means risk management and sales and distribution.

Every single member of Acreage's executive team and board of directors is a white dude. Oh, sorry, all except Larissa Herda, who is a white lady. The drug trade can attract some rough characters, but this has gotta be the first crew to include a former prime minister of Canada (Brian Mulroney), a Republican presidential candidate (William F. Weld), and former Republican Speaker of the House John Boehner.

This is a newly chilled-out Boehner we got here. Back when he was opposing everything Obama tried to do, he didn't seem that into weed. He still doesn't see how his previous leadership in the Republican House helped to put black people in prison. "I don't have any regrets at all," Boehner said recently. "I was opposed to the use of it. The whole criminal justice part of this, frankly, it never crossed my mind."

Overall, decriminalization is good, but I don't think it's enough. I think that you should also give convicts jobs.

Because who knows the weed business better than them? Right? You know how there are certain business schools that the headhunters come and scout you from? Prison should be like that. Why are you going to hire a bunch of white guys for a weed business? Take a look at some of our prisoners: they've already shown proficiency. Prison should be like Wharton for weed.

Reparations Article 51. Weed Wharton

Upon ratification of this treaty, marijuana companies (weed businesses, marijuana holding companies, etc.) shall recruit their executives exclusively from the ranks of those incarcerated for doing an excellent job selling weed previously. This shall be the primary consideration for employment, not being in a hedge fund, investment partnership, management trust, or any other bullshit.

And meanwhile, look at what happens when you have white people like the Sackler family in charge of drug distribution: you get the opioid crisis. So we know that white people in charge of drugs does not work.

WE WANT A JURY OF *OUR* PEERS

White and black people are treated differently by the justice system. Justice is not color blind. Policing is different, sentencing is different, everything's different. But even if cops and prosecutors are biased, juries are supposed to be the people who decide. So here's the thing, because it's really not that complicated: When we have a trial by a jury of our peers, they should actually be our peers. There have to be black people on the jury.

Of course, I'm not saying I want y'all to call me up for jury duty. Last time I got called up, they asked me what justice looked like and I said, "Unfamiliar." They all laughed and then I was off the jury. I can't stop being funny just to help out the justice system, come on now.

When you want to frame up a black guy, you work hard to not have any black people on the jury. In Mississippi, Curtis Flowers, a black man, has been put on trial *six times* for the same crime by the same white prosecutor for a murder in 1996. He's been kept in prison for twenty-two years without a fair conviction.

Theoretically, you're allowed to exclude potential jurors for all sorts of reasons, as long as it's not based on race, sex, or ethnicity. Of course, these "peremptory challenges" are still about race, but the lawyers come up with some other bullshit reason to say why they are striking someone from the jury.

Doug Evans, the prosecutor on this case, has quite a track record:

In the first trial, in 1997, he struck all five black prospective jurors, and then an all-white jury convicted Curtis Flowers and gave him a death sentence. That first trial was overturned because of prosecutorial misconduct.

Nearly the same thing happened at the second trial: Doug Evans tried to strike all the black jurors, but he was only allowed to strike four of the five. So eleven white jurors and one black juror convicted again and again sentenced Curtis to death. Again, the Mississippi Supreme Court reversed it because of prosecutorial misconduct.

It happened again in the third trial! Only one black juror, a conviction, and then the Mississippi Supreme Court overturning the verdict, this time specifically for eliminating jurors based on race.

Fuck, do I have to list the rest of these trials? At the fourth trial, Evans struck as many black jurors as he could, but still had seven white and five black jurors. This jury deadlocked, black versus white, and a mistrial was declared.

The fifth trial also deadlocked, with nine white and three black people.

In the sixth trial, he got a jury of eleven white people and one black person. He did this by asking the black prospective jurors an average of twenty-nine questions each. The white jurors got one question each. This trial led to conviction. In the six trials, sixty-one of the seventy-two jurors were white.

In June 2019, the U.S. Supreme Court ruled that Doug Evans had violated the Constitution. Only two of the justices dissented: Neil Gorsuch and Clarence Thomas, proving once again that he's the worst. Clarence Thomas wrote: "If the court's opinion today has a redeeming quality, it is this: The State is perfectly free to convict Curtis Flowers again."

Curtis was just freed on bail. We'll have to see if Doug Evans tries to convict him again.

When you have black people on a jury, you can even convict cops. It's amazing. Nobody disputes the relevant facts of the Botham Jean murder. Amber Guyger, a white Dallas police officer, shot Botham Jean in his own apartment. She claimed that she was confused and thought she was entering her apartment. Most of the time, juries love to take cops at their word, even if their word makes no sense.

But justice looks different when there are people of color

in the jury box. Juries with black folks have empathy and offer different perspectives than juries without them. In Amber Guyger's trial, there were seven black jurors or alternates, five nonblack people of color, and only four white people. That mix is incredibly rare. In Texas, blacks are only 12 percent of the population, so finding seven black people to serve on a jury doesn't happen a lot.

This jury convicted her of murder and sentenced her to ten years in prison. Ten years for murder is a pretty good deal, especially when you consider the average murderer in America serves seven years. Then again, the average murdered person serves a lifetime.

In one way, I was surprised about the verdict, because usually when white women cry, it has a devastating effect on society. A blond white woman crying is more than people can usually bear. But then I wasn't surprised when I saw who was on the jury, because if there's one group of people who are impervious to white women's tears, it's black women. They're like, "Bitch, come on. Stop with that bullshit."

THE FIGHT FOR CUSTODY

White people: Admit that you don't know how the police treat people different than you. If you're going to put your "Blue Lives Matter" bumper sticker on your car, at least look at the facts about how police act toward black folks. Does it seem like they think black lives matter?

How do you explain how the cops killed Botham Jean, Atatiana Jefferson, and Stephon Clark because they thought they had guns, but took Dylann Roof, Gregory Bush, and Patrick Crusius into custody alive?

Ain't it weird how cops take you alive when they *know* you have a gun, but shoot you dead when they *think* you do? What can explain it?

That's basically how you can tell when the media is talking about a white person. When they say "apprehended" or "in custody," it ain't us.

So, for the purposes of the treaty, we're asking to be taken into custody. We're not saying that black people will never do anything wrong. We're just saying when we do, take us into custody. Don't shoot us.

Reparations Article 5j. Take Us into Custody

Although black people shall endeavor to be blameless in all respects, on the occasion of a dispute wherein the police or other law enforcement shall be called to mediate, we require an expansion of our options. No longer shall police shoot first, having been "scared" or having "perceived a threat." Police shall be required to treat white and black suspects the same, with the option to "apprehend" or "take into custody."

Shootings show what people value. I think it's interesting that right after Dylann Roof murdered nine people in an African American Charleston church, Cecil the lion was also killed. Remember Cecil? He was shot in Zimbabwe by a white dentist out on a trophy hunt. One of those shootings caused people all around the country and the world to send money; Jimmy Kimmel raised $150,000 in donations in less than twenty-four hours. One of those killings caused so much grief that people advocated and made sure that the shooting would never happen again. Not one other lion from that pride has been hunted. Not one other.

So you tell me: What do white people value?

BLACK LIVES MATTER, BUT NOT AS MUCH

Again and again, you prove that black lives don't matter. BLM activism has really irritated white people. It's so in-your-face, so aggressive. Why can't it be more convenient?

You like driving on highways? Sure you do! You got

places to be. I know you don't want some Black Lives Matters activists shutting down the highway when you're trying to get to Target.

And when you watch the big game, do you want more commentary on offensive plays or offensive knee-taking players?

Let me ask you: What's the most convenient protest you've encountered? What's the most memorable *convenient* protest you can think of? Exactly. They're supposed to be inconvenient. The Boston Tea Party was pretty fucked up for the British. I mean, I'm just saying they needed that tea, right? Nobody was like, "Oh, that's okay, I didn't need my teatime today." No. I'm sure people were like, "Where's my fucking tea?" They didn't hold a Boston Baked Beans Party because people would be like, "Eh, I got plenty of beans." But I digress.

This taking-a-knee thing has really gotten to you. Why? Colin Kaepernick is more upsetting than Robert Kraft? Robert Kraft got busted soliciting prostitutes during a sex slavery and human trafficking investigation. So apparently a black man on one knee is too much, but a ho on two is all right.

The point is, we've been trying to get your attention. And the only time white people ever listen to black people is when they're singing, dancing, or running a ball. But what if I promised you that we'd stop all these protests?

The Black Lives Matter movement started to protest police shootings, racism, and white supremacy within the ranks of law enforcement. I hope I don't have to go through all the examples of cops shooting black people for no reason. Didn't you all buy my other book? Come on. It's in paperback now; don't be cheap.

KKKOPS

The Blue Lives Matter crowd wants to pretend that racist cops are hard to find. But there's a million examples of racist behavior from law enforcement when they don't think anyone is listening. Behind closed doors, at home and in private chat rooms and Facebook groups, the thin blue line show their true colors.

Recently a couple was house shopping in Muskegon, Michigan, and they looked at a cop's house, a two-bedroom, one-bath ranch-style. When the couple, both people of color, toured the house with their kids and a Realtor, they came across numerous Confederate flags. They tried to ignore those, because you know—you probably won't keep those if you buy the place. A little paint and wallpaper, maybe. But then they saw the framed KKK application on the wall amid police paraphernalia. So they reported it to the city and the cop was suspended. Now—big surprise—this same cop killed a black man in 2009 "in self-defense." At the time he was cleared of any wrongdoing.

After it was reported, the Muskegon city government opened an investigation into the 2009 shooting as well as other incidents. So it takes the Property Brothers to get people to look into police shootings.

My real estate broker told me to put my family photos away, and this guy thought it was okay to have his KKK shit out? I mean, you gotta really think the Klan's okay if you're gonna let people see it on your house tour. That's some next-level racist shit. All you gotta do is watch a little HGTV to know that you don't stage your house for sale with KKK memorabilia. That's House-Selling 101. Put out some fresh-baked cookies, repaint a bit, and clear out the clutter. Replace that old couch. Maybe buy a new slipcover, or better yet just use one of your robes.

Even when they aren't KKK-Kard Karrying members, too many police and law enforcement officers are at least KKK-Kurious. They may not be members of white nationalist groups, but they agree with them. When's the last time a white nationalist did something and you saw policemen outraged? Yet you've seen them have to be restrained because a black motorist asked them what they'd been pulled over for. Have you ever seen them having to be restrained that way after a guy just slaughtered twenty people?

The way I see it, there's a symbiotic relationship between white supremacists and law enforcement. They have some of the same interests and the same views—i.e., protecting the powers that be. They're cozy. It's not hard to imagine that a lot of police officers have more in common with white nationalists than with a black dude who lives in the city, right?

And when we get a peek at their private conversations, that's borne out. In 2016, San Francisco PD officers got caught texting each other racist messages. One text message featured the image of a badly burned turkey and the words "Is that a Ferguson turkey?" One of those cops went on to rob a couple of banks, so you know he might have also had money problems.

In Philadelphia, seventy-two officers were reassigned after a reporting database, the Plain View Project, published some of their racist posts. The same project published a post from a Phoenix officer: "It's a good day for a chokehold." More than fifty police departments opened investigations of officers after Reveal from the Center for Investigative Reporting reported on racist, Islamophobic, and violent posts.

When Eric Garner was choked to death by an officer for selling "loosies," the officers on the scene texted their commander that "He's most likely DOA." The commander's reply? "Not a big deal."

When that detail was read aloud at a police disciplinary hearing for Officer Daniel Pantaleo, there was an audible gasp in the courtroom. And I don't think that gasp was from shock. I think that gasp was from realizing, "Oh shit, they have our text messages!" *Can they do that?*

And it's not just police. A Facebook group for Border Protection agents was found to be full of racist memes and violent imagery. The chief of Customs and Border Protection was herself a member of the group.

But do police departments really have a white supremacy problem? The FBI thought so. The FBI investigated the infiltration of police departments by white supremacy groups and issued a report in 2006, finding that "white supremacist leaders and groups have historically shown an interest in infiltrating law enforcement communities or recruiting law enforcement personnel." And again in 2015, the FBI reported that "domestic terrorism investigations focused on militia extremists, white supremacist extremists, and sovereign citizen extremists often have identified active links to law enforcement officers."

Despite this report, nobody's done much to address this threat.

And even though the presence of white supremacists in law enforcement has been exposed as being very active in the Trump era, the FBI has instead focused its sights on different threats: "Black Identity Extremists," basically a made-up idea.

As detailed in an FBI Intelligence Assessment Report, "The FBI assesses it is very likely Black Identity Extremist (BIE) perceptions of police brutality against African Americans spurred an increase in premeditated, retaliatory lethal violence against law enforcement and will very likely serve as justification for such violence." This came out around the same time that white supremacists were gathering in Charlottesville. And the FBI's 2018–19 "Threat Guidance" documents describe BIEs as those who "use force or violence in violation of criminal law in response to perceived racism and injustice in American society." These BIEs were perceived to be a major threat, higher than Al Qaeda or white supremacists.

So it's black extremists, then Al Qaeda, then white supremacists? I guess dudes in dashikis are scarier than dudes with torches? It's a weird world.

By 2019, the FBI decided to scrap the term "Black Identity Extremist" and fold it into a "Racially Motivated Extremism" category that includes both "White Racially Motivated Extremism, previously referred to as White Supremacy Extremism, and Black Racially Motivated Extremism, previously referred to as Black Identity Extremism." But here we go again, pretending that the threat from white supremacists must also have a black counterpart, when in reality there is no organized "Black Identity Extremist" movement. The few isolated examples of violence against cops don't make it a movement.

Inconvenient protests against police brutality don't constitute a "War on Cops." Protests *against* racism aren't a racist movement for *black* supremacy. That's more "both sides are to blame" nonsense.

This is another example of where helping us helps you. You don't want the FBI wasting money and resources on made-up threats. You want them to be stopping the next mass shooter, not the guys at the drum circle in the park.

All we're asking is, how is it okay for cops to say shit on Facebook that would get you fired anywhere? If you worked at White Castle and said, "Fuck the niggers," you'd at least be put on fry duty. Where's the HR department at the PD? And you don't get to carry a gun at White Castle, though too many sliders can be deadly.

In fact, that's a good way to judge it. I have more faith in the White Castle HR department than the police department. So we're gonna let White Castle decide. We'll call it the White Castle Doctrine. We'll run whatever you say by White Castle HR and see if they have a problem with it. "Go back to Africa," or "Why are we having all these people from shithole countries come here?"—we'll just check with WC HR, and if they say it's fine, then we're cool.

Reparations Article 5k. The White Castle Doctrine

Due to the historic infiltration of law enforcement by racists and white supremacists, and in consideration of the fact that White Castle serves up food without calling anyone the N-word, we now require personnel decisions to be made by the White Castle human resources department, until such a time as racists are rooted out of the police, border security, and so on. In the event of a dispute, White Castle HR can ask Taco Bell HR to arbitrate.

Once the last racist is purged from the PD, we'll stop making a fuss. You can watch the football players smash each other without ever having to think about violence. The only kneeling will be by the cooler in the parking lot. And you can enjoy your highways without any protesters getting in the way, as long as Trump passes that big infrastructure plan, that is.

In the meantime, how can we give the benefit of the doubt to police forces that harass us, lie to us, turn off their body cameras, text each other racist things, and then say they "felt threatened"? If feeling threatened were a reason you could kill someone, y'all'd be dead already.

We're supposed to believe Amber Guyger had no bias, and yet she'd been texting racist things to her boyfriend, a cop she was having an affair with, who had killed an unarmed black person in 2008?

In Fort Worth, the officer shot Atatiana Jefferson through the window after cops had been creeping around in her backyard without announcing themselves, but white people treat that like it's an aberration instead of a point on a continuum. Look at it in context. A year before, a black woman was with her kid and the kid dropped a raisin on the ground, and some white guy living there came and knocked her son over. When the cops arrived, they took the assailant's side, saying, "Why don't you teach him not to litter?" What explains an attitude like that, except bias?

A white woman at a Fort Worth city council meeting after the shooting told everyone about how the cops had been skulking around in her backyard on a different call. And all she was worried about was that they might hurt her dog. That's white privilege. That's the difference between worrying about your dog and worrying about your life.

The police are different in your neighborhoods. I can always tell how dark the neighborhood is by how long it takes the police to get there. Police precincts generally pride themselves on their response time, but in black neighborhoods there's no rush. And generally, in our neighborhoods, they're not coming to stop shit or arrest anybody. They're coming just to draw chalk or put up the yellow tape, so it doesn't really require a rapid response.

And any black person who calls the police knows that 911 is hairy. They know it's a dangerous situation—they need help, but they might not like the "help" they get. Black people who need help know that there's a certain protocol we have to have. So Atatiana Jefferson's neighbor, who was worried about her door being open, called a nonemergency line for a wellness check. The cops never identified themselves, walked right past the door and into the backyard. When Jefferson came to the window, one of the officers yelled, "Show me your hands!" and shot her in four seconds.

STAY PUT

Botham Jean got shot because Officer Amber Guyger went into *his* apartment. Atatiana Jefferson got shot because Officer Aaron Dean was creeping around *her* backyard. And it's always the same argument: they shot because they were *afraid*. How does the same excuse work for Eric Garner as works for Botham Jean? How does the same excuse work for Michael Brown and Atatiana Jefferson?

Because when you're black or brown, they don't just kill you. They kill your reputation. So you die more than one time. You know the old expression "a coward dies a thousand deaths"? So does a black man. They kill him, then they kill who he was, his reputation, the idea of him, his life's work.

How is it possible for *us* to die when white people are in the wrong place? It used to be we'd get killed when we were in the wrong place. Now, we get killed when white people are.

White people need to stop traveling so fucking much. When white people get lost and kill people of color, they get a holiday, like Columbus. White people in the wrong place cost black and brown people their lives, and always have.

Why don't you slow down? Settle down somewhere. Horace Greeley said, "Go west, young man." You've gone far enough! Plant some roots. Stay put.

Whenever Trump is accused by somebody of something, the first thing that he does is see what their affiliations are. "Oh, they voted for Hillary," or "They're part of the Deep State," or "They're a Democrat." As if someone who's not like him or who dislikes him must be unbiased. And his base buys it. He's convinced people that others lack the impartiality to be fair based on who they vote for or what they believe or who they like and dislike.

So I agree with him for once. I agree that it is impossible for somebody who doesn't like you to be fair. I agree. The problem is that the real Deep State is the deep state of racism in the police departments in America. One man's rogue cop is another man's Robert Mueller.

But I think racists gotta eat too, right? I think you can be a racist cop. I just don't think you should ever be a racist cop in our neighborhoods. Like, if you're a racist in your neighborhoods but don't ever leave there, I don't care. But don't come on over into anywhere black people live or work.

So I think racist cops should have a monitoring bracelet. You know, maybe an ankle bracelet that alerts black people if you go past the perimeter. That way you get to keep your job and you don't get sacked. It's like those dogs with invisible fences: you see them bark and bark, but they never cross the line, or they get a little shock. Racist cops get a little charge and that way black people don't get falsely charged.

Because we can't root out all the racist cops. What we can do is stop them from shitting in other people's yards.

Look at it this way: Wherever you white folks go, you get fucking scared. You overreact. Stay at home! You know how when there's an active shooter incident they tell you to "shelter in place"? Well, we're asking you to "shelter in place" so you don't become an active shooter of us.

You've got nice houses; you live in nice neighborhoods. Enjoy those homes you paid for. Stay in tonight. "Netflix and chill" means no niggas die.

Reparations Article 51. Stay Put

Whenever white people wander around, black and brown people die. Now that there are multiple streaming platforms, there's no need to go out quite so much. Stay home, enjoy a night in so that we may also enjoy a night in or out. White people, especially cops, are hereby ordered to stay in and binge-watch some of the new offerings on Apple TV+ or Hulu before they start going around exploring, and possibly killing.

WE ARE PART OF AMERICA

We're not going anywhere. As such, we demand full access to America, with full rights and privileges thereof.

WE'RE PART OF AMERICA

Come to think of it, white people wandering all over has been a particular problem for black people since the beginning. White people brought us here to America in 1619, and yet you still treat us like we aren't a real part of America.

GO BACK TO WHERE YOU CAME FROM

Anytime a person of color raises an objection about this country, white people say, "Go back where you came from. Go back to Africa." But everybody knows you can't return stolen goods.

YOUR TIRED, YOUR POOR NEED NOT APPLY

The American Dream used to mean the opportunity to build yourself up from nothing into *something*. That was the promise and that's the story so many white conservatives like to tell themselves about their own families: *My ancestor came over with a nickel in his pocket and built himself into something.*

But now, white people are trying to close the door. And even people here *legally* are having their status revoked because of the discriminatory, white-supremacist policies of the Trump administration. One such rule takes away green cards or visas if Immigration Services feels a legal immigrant is likely to use government benefits.

Ken Cuccinelli, the acting director of U.S. Citizenship and Immigration Services, defended this change. He was asked how to reconcile this with the poem on the Statue of Liberty, "The New Colossus," which says, "Give me your tired, your poor, your huddled masses yearning to breathe free." He restated it as "Give me your tired and your poor who can stand on their own two feet and who will not become a public charge." You don't get to rewrite history like that—the poem says:

> *"Keep, ancient lands, your storied pomp!" cries she*
> *With silent lips. "Give me your tired, your poor,*
> *Your huddled masses yearning to breathe free,*
> *The wretched refuse of your teeming shore.*
> *Send these, the homeless, tempest-tost to me,*
> *I lift my lamp beside the golden door!"*

If you're poor, you're not standing on your own two feet. If you're "wretched refuse," you might need some help. If you're homeless and "tempest-tost," you might need a housing voucher. That's the promise of America: You can start from nothing and become something. Not start from something and become something.

And because this guy can't leave well enough alone, he claimed that the "wretched refuse" was referring to "people coming from Europe." Well, that's interesting, because the Statue of Liberty was actually a gift from France to celebrate the abolition of slavery. As a matter of fact, the original designs had her holding broken shackles in her left hand. In the final version, she has broken chains at her feet. When's the last time white people needed to break chains? I mean, *Cool Hand Luke* was the last time white people had chains on. *"I'm shaking that bush, boss! I'm shakin' it!"* That was the last time.

So that's another thing we want: Be honest about history. You can't rewrite history, just like you can't rewrite "The New Colossus." According to Cuccinelli and people like him, his family has an incredible, noble story of how they came to this country that's *totally different* from the stories of the black and brown immigrants coming over now. It's always this great tale about how their grandfather came over here with nothing to his name and pulled himself up by his bootstraps. I always feel like it's the same dude, because it's always the same story. It's like they all had the same grandfather. *He didn't speak a word of English, he had a single nickel in his pocket, and he opened up a salami shop.* It's the same story! Either they're lying or they've got the same grandfather.

Anyway, the point is that people coming here *now* with nothing aren't any different from people who came over *then* with nothing. The restrictions people like Cuccinelli are trying to put in place *now* would have excluded his own relatives *then*. Southern Italians without any money or education like Cuccinelli's great-grandparents were just the kind of parasites that people would have gladly sent home at the time. Ken's great-grandfather came through Ellis Island with $8.75 in 1901. He worked as a laborer and by 1905 was supporting a family of six. Ken's great-grandmother came through Ellis Island in 1903 and was detained there as an "L.P.C.": "Likely Public Charge." She was literally labeled as a likely public charge, just like the "public charges" Ken Cuccinelli hopes to ban *right now*.

Nobody ever tells a white person to go back to where they came from. "Go back to Canada. Go back to Ireland. Go back to Italy." It doesn't happen. We have to be able to call things racist when they are. Not everything, but certain things we all agree are racist, like when Donald Trump said, "Go back where you came from." Why don't you go back to Germany? Or was it Sweden, like he said in *The Art of the Deal*? That's where Donald used to say his grandfather Frederick, originally Friedrich, was from. Huh. And why would Trump's father, Fred Trump, not own up to that? Why would a guy want to say his family was from Sweden, not Germany, when he was trying to sell real estate to Jews in New York?

Weirdly, Friedrich Trump *did* try to "go back where he came from" a couple of times. Germany wouldn't take him back because they thought he had tried to avoid military service by moving to America. Friedrich wanted to return, saying, "We are loyal Germans and stand behind the high Kaiser and the mighty German Reich." But the Germans wouldn't restore his citizenship. Donald's father, Fred, might have grown up in Germany instead of in Queens, if only Germany hadn't been so picky. Can you blame them?

So it takes some fucking nerve to tell black people to "go back to where they came from" when their families have been here a lot longer than Trump's. Black people loved America when America didn't love us.

The reason white people now have a problem with America is because it looks different than they thought it did. They're just now really getting to know America, and they don't like her. We've always known her.

WE'RE NOT REALLY PART OF AMERICA

Right now, we're not really part of America. We've got a holiday and some streets named after Martin Luther King Jr. That's it. They ran out of famous white people to name shit after, so they started in on unknown white dudes. I went to Robert E. Peary High. Nobody knew who the fuck he was. It turns out that his claim to fame is that he *almost* made it to the North Pole. He gets a school before a black dude who actually *did* something? (Or how about at least showing love to Peary's African American partner on the North Pole expedition, Matthew Henson?)

And all the schools and buildings and parks are named after white people who didn't like us. All over America, we go to schools named after people who hated us and barbecue in parks with statues of people who hated us. Why do we still have to deal with it? How many elementary schools are named for black people? How many high schools? We want to share America.

Even in the 2020 primaries, the Democrats ignored black people until we showed up in South Carolina and made them listen. Black people did not get their say until the nearly all-white voters of Iowa and New Hampshire had set the narrative. But South Carolina is basically Black Iowa. And black people said: We don't want Bernie Sanders, we want Joe Biden. We want the guy we know, who had our dude's back.

We want our share. We're not visitors. We're ingrained in America. White people do as little as they can to make us feel really a part of America. We've been here four hundred years. We have been here longer than the people telling us to go back.

FASHION VICTIMS

Here's what happens when you don't include black people: you get fuckups like Gucci putting out an $800 turtleneck sweater with blackface-style lips on it, then Katy Perry putting out shoes with big red Sambo-style lips, only a few months after Prada attached little golliwog-style dolls to its bags.

When Burberry sends a model down the runway with a noose around her neck, it doesn't mean that the KKK has an inside man with fashion sense. I mean, take one look at the Charlottesville dudes in their Trump khakis and polo shirts and you know there's no fashion sense in white supremacy. So I don't think the people at Burberry or Prada are inherently racist, I just think no black people are in the fucking room to say, "Hey, that's a bad idea."

Burberry defended itself by saying the rope was part of a nautical theme, and okay, sure, if you had a bowline or a clove hitch on a model, maybe that's fine. Bowlines are as nautical as a motherfucking sailor's cap. But you wouldn't look at that noose and think, *Oh, sure, it's just some Jacques Cousteau shit.* An upside-down loop hanging around someone's neck? That's a noose. And a noose is a no-no knot. A knot-knot no? You know what I mean.

Whenever white people get together in private, it's never good for black people. I don't care if it's a jury, I don't care if it's an Oscar nomination. Whenever white people get to close a curtain, it never goes good for anybody. The best thing would be to make sure that there are people of color in the room. That's the main thing. But until that time, we've gotta get rid of America's curtains.

Reparations Article 6a. It's Curtains for Curtains

White people can have sheer curtains only. Full transparency means full transparency. Maybe you can have those beaded curtains. But no drapes. Venetian blinds are okay, as long as they are partway open. You can use shutters the same way, because we know you all love those. Wiping out prejudice and bias will take time, and until then we want to keep an eye on you all. Justice is blind. Justice has blinds.

Fashion's always pushing the edge, but it shouldn't take 50 Cent burning his Gucci to get people to put some black folks in the room. And still, the fashion people fucked up. Chanel's first head of diversity is Fiona Pargeter, a white woman. Why the hell would you hire a white woman to be the head of diversity?

And maybe you can chalk up some of this to the fact that some of these brands are Italian or French and don't totally understand the nuances of racist imagery in America. But still, you're gonna let some old Italian guy decide what is okay to put out in America?

A lot of these brands don't really advertise as much as they rely on dope black celebrities to wear their clothes, showcasing them on TV, Instagram, and so on. Gucci ain't Aflac; they don't do commercials. What they do is LeBron. And still a lot of black people can't afford the things they see, so they go to get the closest approximation: it ain't Prada, but it's Zara. Regardless, I think that the fashion industry should give us black people a discount for acting as models and for making even cheap knockoffs look dope. So, since black people were considered three-fifths human, we should only have to pay three-fifths the price. That's like $2,000 Prada or $12.50 Zara. You're welcome.

Racist imagery isn't something we made up. It's baked into the bread in America. Aunt Jemima traded her "mammy" bandanna for a headband in 1968 and got a perm in the '80s, but she's still an old stereotype. Uncle Ben and "Rastus," the Cream of Wheat chef, are still on boxes at the supermarket, even if you can't buy Darkie toothpaste anymore. Why do black people still gotta look at the same motherfucker who said, "Maybe Cream of Wheat ain't got no vitamines. I don't know what them things is. If they's bugs they aint none in Cream of Wheat." I'm just waking up; I don't need to think about this shit so early.

So, okay, you still want to eat fucking pancakes, right? Fine. But we gotta set some rules. No more bullshit.

FIT THE BILL

So we can be a cook in the kitchen, but there's not one single black person on money.

Just before Obama left office, they were going to put Harriet Tubman on the twenty-dollar bill, replacing Andrew Jackson. Then it was announced that she'd be put on the back, but Andrew Jackson would stay on the front. It was too much to get rid of Andrew Jackson. Never mind how weird it is that a woman who helped hundreds of people escape slavery would be sharing a bill with a man who owned hundreds of slaves. I've shared some weird bills while touring on the road, but damn.

A slave on one side, a slave owner on the other. So even

when black people make it to money, we've still got a supervisor. *All right, Harriet, break's over. Time to get back to work.*

Predictably, the Trump administration "delayed" her twenty-dollar bill until at least 2026, after Trump is out of office. Or maybe never. Trump loves Jackson: "Andrew Jackson had a great history, and I think it's very rough when you take somebody off the bill." Rednecks don't want a black woman on their money.

But we're part of America, so we want more split bills.

- **ONE-DOLLAR BILL:** George Washington / George Washington Carver
- **FIVE-DOLLAR BILL:** Abe Lincoln / maybe no one; it feels rude to have someone come up behind Abe, given his history.
- **TEN-DOLLAR BILL:** Alexander Hamilton / Lin-Manuel Miranda

And Harriet gets her own bill.

IMAGINARY PEOPLE CAN BE BLACK

I always say that the most dangerous place for black people to live is in white people's imaginations. But damn, we're not even *allowed* to live in white people's imaginations.

Disney announced that Halle Bailey was gonna be Ariel

in a new live-action remake of *The Little Mermaid,* and of course everybody got mad because *how could the Little Mermaid be black?* Which is weird because she's an imaginary character. She's not real, there was no real Ariel. It's imaginary. You can't even let us be an imaginary character? Black people didn't get mad when they made that crab Jamaican. That shit is not real.

Or Santa. Kids, close your eyes—don't read this next part . . . We good?

Santa is not *real.* There is no Santa. But tell that to the people who got all agitated over the Mall of America having a black Santa in 2016. What is it about a black Santa that freaks you out? Yeah, normally he looks like a white guy, but we can't have *any* black Santas? You don't think a black dude can have a little round belly that shakes like a bowlful of jelly? Al Roker slimmed down, but I still know some heavy dudes. You don't need to see white skin to know it's Santa. If you see *any* guy in a red suit, you're probably looking at a Santa. It's not hard to figure it out. As the Mall of America's Santa Larry himself said, "It's no big deal, I'm still Santa, I just happen to be a Santa of Color." No big deal, but then again, a black Santa's gonna have to be a lot more careful breaking into people's houses with a sack of gifts.

Or 007—*Bond, James Bond*—is not real. Idris Elba would

be a kickass Bond, a natural choice. But some people can't handle a black Bond. The writer of the newest Bond novel said Idris Elba is "too street" to be Bond. A black dude in a dope car? That's our brand. You believe that Bond can shoot a rocket out of a boom box or have X-ray sunglasses, but being a black guy is too incredible? In *Goldfinger,* Bond put a duck on his head so he could swim into an enemy base. And yet a duck hat is more believable than a black Bond.

And you know, it's fucked up that you want to keep imaginary characters white when you've already made black imaginary characters white, like Jesus.

Reparations Article 6b. Invisible Men

Henceforth there shall be inclusion and diversity in the realm of the imaginary, the made-up, and the fantastical. There are real black people and there shall thus be unreal black people. The world of make-believe, science fiction, fantasy, and any other genre of fancy, reverie, or invention shall be open to black imaginary people. This shall include but not be limited to imaginary friends, fictional characters, spies, phantoms, and ghosts.

DON'T WRITE US OUT OF THE FUTURE

Unlike a lot of white people who blame brown people, I know that it's robots that are taking white people's jobs.

Robots and computers can do almost anything that a person can do, only quicker and with less complaining. Lucky for me, robots are horrible at telling jokes: *Why was the robot mad? Because people kept pushing his buttons.* See? That shit is terrible. I ain't worried until they get down comedy's *nuts and bolts*. But I digress.

Robots aren't going anywhere, so we gotta make sure they're programmed right, because people's biases are being built into technology. Y'all shut us out of the past; we gotta make sure we're not written out of the future. It's bad enough dealing with racist people, but robots? I just saw *Child's Play 2* and that serial killer dude input his personality into that Chucky doll, and before you know it, he's beating some teacher to death with a yardstick. Robots could be even worse.

Maybe you've seen the viral videos of "racist automatic soap dispensers" that dish out soap to white hands but not black or brown hands? The sensor on the dispensers isn't detecting the light bouncing off of black skin, so *NO SOAP FOR YOU.* I usually have to wait for a white guy to start washing his hands and then I'll stick my hands under. Used to be you'd have a black bathroom attendant to hand you a towel, but now we need a white guy just to get the soap started.

Now, nobody's gonna die from not washing their hands. Oh shit, actually . . . Personally, I'm not worried about the coronavirus because there's never been an epidemic so bad that everyone was okay with a bunch of niggas wearing masks. If it gets to that point, they will find a cure. But the people who programmed this thing: probably not a bunch of black dudes. That's 'cause there aren't that many black people working in tech. In 2018, Facebook was only 3 percent black, Google only 2 percent. That's typical and it causes errors like this.

And the same thing happens with facial recognition cameras: a study by MIT and Stanford found an error rate of less than 1 percent for light-skinned men and almost 35 percent for dark-skinned women. Because we all look alike? According to the robots, yes. That discrepancy affects all sorts of systems, from security cameras to image-sorting applications. In Brooklyn, a facial recognition program was introduced in a housing complex to use instead of keys. A robot that doesn't recognize you can lock you out of your home: "Open the doors, HAL." *I'm sorry, Dave. I'm afraid I can't do that.*

And in Detroit, real-time police cameras have been installed at two public housing projects. Isn't it weird that they put these cameras in black communities first? These systems are getting rolled out everywhere, but if the bias is built into them from the start, it's just another way for police to target people of color. Misidentified people end up in a system that can be checked by the police, searched, and scanned for people who "fit the description."

I don't trust the police and I don't trust robocops. People are getting arrested on the basis of facial recognition matching alone. In one example, the NYPD ran a picture of Woody Harrelson through a program after a victim said a suspect looked like him. "This celebrity 'match' was sent back to the investigating officers, and someone who was not Woody Harrelson was eventually arrested for petit larceny," the report said. Granted, Woody Harrelson is sketchy-looking as hell. But I don't want the cops using my headshot in a lineup. *Yes, officer, he looked just like my favorite comedian, D.L. Hughley.*

And once you get arrested, your sentence might get determined by an algorithm that's programmed against you.

ProPublica did a study of risk assessment programs that are used by judges to determine sentencing. In their study of these risk scores in Broward County, Florida, they found that the formula was likely to flag black defendants as "likely to repeat offend" at a much higher rate than white defendants. And it underestimated risk scores for white defendants. These sorts of biased systems are used all over the country, and nobody's accountable for their results or their accuracy—except the black people who get put in prison because of them. I didn't know *Minority Report* was just about reporting minorities.

It ain't all bad news for black people, though. Apparently, pretty soon you can have Samuel L. Jackson be the voice for your Alexa. Look how far we've come, right? Now we got black robots! But do you know how many people are gonna call the police when they hear "This nigga wants to play the Rolling Stones"—*Wait, wait it's just my Alexa, don't shoot!*

We've gone from whipping black people when they speak to making them our robot voices in a few generations. So it's great that Sam Jackson's the voice of Alexa, but that's not enough progress.

CONCLUSION

So that's really it. I know some past treaties you all have signed have gone bad, like:

1778—Treaty with the Delawares

1782—Chickasaw Peace Treaty Feeler

1784—Treaty with the Six Nations

1785—Treaty with the Wyandot, Etc.

1785—Treaty with the Cherokee

1786—Treaty with the Choctaw

17 . . . you get the idea.

But I feel like this one will stick. I got a good feeling about this one. Do these things and we'll shut the fuck up:

THE OFFICIAL TREATY ENDING
THE 400-YEAR CONFLICT BETWEEN
AMERICA AND PEOPLE OF COLOR

Preamble: A Peace Treaty Between
White America and Black Folks

The search for peace between races must be guided by the following:

Black folks ("African Americans," "people of color," "those people") have decided, after four hundred years of oppression and discrimination, to come to the table and issue demands for a lasting peace with their oppressors. That's mighty big of them.

White people ("America"), having determined to hold a conference with the black folks, for the purpose of removing from their minds all causes of complaint, making them stop grousing, posting annoying memes to social media, and otherwise throwing shade, and establishing a firm and permanent friendship with them, recognize D.L. Hughley as sole agent for that purpose and affirm their intent to come to terms.

Recognizing that it is in the interest of all that racial harmony be established and racial animus shall no longer be the default;

Acknowledging that cooperation in this goal is of the essence and necessary, that peace may prosper, even if that means talking about things that upset the apple cart;

Acknowledging also that everyone's been a little hot under the collar for a while about all this stuff;

Convinced that the establishment of a firm foundation for the continuation and development of such cooperation on the basis of mutual understanding accords with the interests of harmony and peace;

Convinced also that a treaty ensuring this peace, by nature, must be specific and must cut the treacle;

Now, in order to accomplish the good design of this conference, the parties have agreed on the following articles, which, when ratified, shall be fully binding.

ARTICLE I: WHITE PEOPLE SHALL CONSIDER REPARATIONS

Despite the protests of Mitch McConnell and other white conservatives, a good-faith effort shall be made to make amends to black people. Just like the Italians and Japanese, we want an apology, if not a little walking-around money. Furthermore:

REPARATIONS ARTICLE 1A. CHICKEN DISCOUNT

It is thus decided that due to the Popeyes chicken sandwich being much beloved in the black community, but in suspiciously short supply, all such sandwiches shall be offered to black folks at a three-fifths discount.

Reparations Article 1b. Nipsey Hall

In recognition of the fact that buildings are named after old white guys, some of whom were involved in the very systemic racism and oppression that have brought us to this fraught moment of racial tension, we hereby establish a new naming criterion for buildings in universities, cities, and other public institutions. Consideration shall be given to badass, dope niggas whose time passed too soon and who might not previously have been accepted as people to bear in tribute.

Article II: History Books Shall Be Aligned

In order for black folks and white people to further understand one another, our history books must be aligned with the facts, agreed upon by both parties and taken into account.

Article III: We Shall Endeavor to Understand One Another

As we come to live together more and more, conflicts ensue and must be defused. We must attempt to understand each other and our motives. Furthermore:

Reparations Article 3a. Statute of Statue Limitations

White people having gotten overly attached to bronze statues of racists, and having erected statues anywhere they could in an effort to remind black people of who was in charge, now agree to end the practice of erecting new bronze statues. Bronze, a possibly racist alloy, will be replaced as a building material by plaster of Paris, Play-Doh, or some other temporary building material. New statues will be limited to a seven-year erection, which is more than you need anyway, in most instances.

REPARATIONS ARTICLE 3B.
BLACKFACE FOR WHITE FOLKS

White people, having embraced blackface as a fun dress-up tool, having enjoyed Halloween parties in the 1980s, having engaged in racist skits during fraternity parties of the 1990s, and having celebrated such problematic frivolity by documenting black-face in uncountable yearbook pages, shall henceforth be held blameless. Their love of Michael Jackson is hereby affirmed, and their right to wear blackface is retained. This privilege is restricted, however, to Election Day, bank loan interviews, and any other occasion where historical discrimination against people of color has been exhibited.

REPARATIONS ARTICLE 3C.
BLACK EYES FOR THE WHITE GUY

It is thus decided, Hollywood's top writers and producers must be brought together in pursuit of a relatable black comedy or makeover show for the masses. We need some of that creativity put in service of making people like us more. We want some shit on Netflix, on NBC, heck, even something that can run on CBS to catch some old white people after *NCIS*.

REPARATIONS ARTICLE 3D. DON'T CALL ME THE N-WORD WHILE I'M EATING

Racism has no place in America, and certainly not in a Buffalo Wild Wings or a Papa John's. Herewith, black people shall eat in peace, without having to deal with slurs and antagonism. Polite dinner conversation only, please.

REPARATIONS ARTICLE 3E. WE KEEP MAC AND CHEESE AND HALL AND OATES

Lest the foodstuffs and music much adored by all peoples become the subject of continuous wrangling and conflict, we heresoforwith declare cultural appropriation to be approved for use by all peoples. Just don't be a big jerk about it.

REPARATIONS ARTICLE 3F. BING ONLY

In consideration of Google's accurate search results, which serve only to dredge up true, horrible, unpleasant facts that make white people feel bad, all black people are hereby sentenced to use Bing only for searches, so that the information is less true, less accurate, and less painful.

REPARATIONS ARTICLE 3G.
WE GET TO BE AVERAGE

Until such a time as the number of average black folks equals the number of average white folks in positions of power, acclaim, and wealth, black people shall herewith be allowed to be "normal," "average," and "unremarkable" without being deemed deficient. Until such a time as the amount of "remarkable" white people in charge of things, held up for praise, or otherwise regarded as successful increases, black people shall enjoy the same respect for being average as their white peers, suffering no penalty.

REPARATIONS ARTICLE 3H. TAKE KANYE

Kanye is yours. He's an honorary white guy now. Since he likes to hang out with Trump so much and spout a bunch of crazy nonsense all the time, we trade him to you.

REPARATIONS ARTICLE 3I.
WHITE BLACK PEOPLE

On the condition that you live like a black person but are in all other respects white, if you're forgotten, ignored, disrespected, economically disadvantaged, picked on, and stressed, you are henceforth, for all intents and purposes, a black person.

Reparations Article 3j. If You're Black, You're Black, Unless You're Not

Excluding those already denoted by name (Kanye et al.), if you are black, you are black. No trading in your blackness until we've sorted this whole thing out.

Reparations Article 3k. Personal Days

All holidays must herewith be evaluated as a whole; i.e., all holidays will be put on a probationary period to ascertain their relevance and value to all Americans. Acknowledging that days off are nice and that mattress sales must occur, a number of holidays shall be continued, but no current holiday will by reason of tradition be kept without scrutiny. MLK Day excluded, because you already tried to take that shit away.

Article IV: We Shall Deal with the White Supremacy Problem

White supremacy, a loathsome American tradition, must be dealt with. Furthermore:

Reparations Article 4a. Full Employment for Racists

Acknowledging that "idle hands are the devil's playthings," and in consideration of the long history of idle racists stirring up trouble, ascribing their woes to the gainfully employed of other races, all efforts shall be made to keep racists employed, with job training to put their "skills" to good use.

Reparations Article 4b. Jesus in Da Club

To restore historical accuracy to the Jesus beloved by white nationalists and black folk alike, and to hopefully make Jesus a bit more accountable to everyone, regardless of the color of their skin, blond-haired, blue-eyed Jesuses shall henceforth be replaced with black Jesuses, modeled after 50 Cent. Jesus will still have abs, just black abs. Also, when there's a manger scene: let's get some black sheep up in that shit too.

Article V: We Shall Be Un-Oppressed

In America, we are still oppressed. In housing and wealth we are left behind. In health, we suffer. The South is still a big fucking problem. In justice and policing, we are discriminated against and abused. This oppression must be countered and lifted! Furthermore:

Reparations Article 5a. Sailing Season-Ticket Holders

All supporters of sports of dubious import, the sole purpose of which is admitting their children into college, shall be subject to season-pass requirements. Archery, rowing, fencing, jousting, dressage, or any other stupid sport shall be canceled if there are not enough white parents in attendance at the matches. In addition, every white season-ticket holder for an NCAA basketball or football team shall also be a season-ticket holder for the water polo team.

REPARATIONS ARTICLE 5B. PAY UP, OR RUGBY

The sport of rugby, being abhorrent in nature, undesirable to both black and white, who do both enjoy the Sundays spent watching "the Big Game," shall henceforth be set aside in favor of keeping black athletes playing ball. Black athletes will play ball if white supporters will likewise play ball, financing historically black colleges and universities, paying athletes their worth, and generally respecting the fact that nobody would give a fuck about Alabama without Tua Tagovailoa.

REPARATIONS ARTICLE 5C.
TRUTH IN ADVERTISING

White people, being beneficiaries of racist housing policies, having written the rules to ensure all-white suburbs, and having extended opportunity to whites only, shall henceforth retain their cherished lies about the lack of privilege and opportunity that they had. Not having lacked for privilege and opportunity, they shall nonetheless henceforth have the privilege and opportunity of lack: that is, they shall retain the opportunity to say they did not have much, grew up in humble circumstances, are self-made in every way. However, if a place is named in such recollections, if an anecdote of their upbringing is in the offing, they must amend the place-name with the preface "All-White" to bring a bit of truth to the lie.

REPARATIONS ARTICLE 5D. TAKE IT EASY PASS

Until such a time as highways are put through white neighborhoods, and in consideration of the inequal use of eminent domain, the building of highway projects in black neighborhoods, and the drawbacks that accrue therefrom, black people shall be issued Easy Passes that provide discounted (free) tolls for all highways.

REPARATIONS ARTICLE 5E.
NEAR OUR HOUSES: ACTUAL FOOD

We need actual food in our neighborhoods: quality grocery stores with fresh fruit, vegetables, and meats. For the purposes of this agreement, neither a pile of bananas by the cash register nor any meat in a can shall constitute "fresh," regardless of the packaging's claims. We want real restaurants and coffee shops; the McCafé section of a McDonald's shall not count. We want environmental justice, so that we don't have to use Fabuloso to scrub out the pollutants in our homes. We want that fresh pine smell and that fresh clean air you all got.

REPARATIONS ARTICLE 5F.
BLACK NEIGHBORHOOD REHAB

It's makeover time for black neighborhoods, due to the lead pipes and paint. We hereby demand that the HGTV network send some of their experts in to get the lead out and spruce the place up, preferably that Chip and Joanna couple, as long as Chip keeps the corny jokes to a minimum. If they are busy, we'll take the Property Brothers.

REPARATIONS ARTICLE 5G.
STAY RACIST, MEDICALLY

White people, unable to eliminate racism and bias in all forms, are hereby allowed to remain racist in matters of pre-scribing medicine, especially opioids and pain medications. With expanded access to health care, we understand that risks to us increase, but we'll worry about that when y'all approve Obamacare's Medicaid expansion anywhere in the South at all. In the meantime, if a wealthy black person requires pain meds, please remember that he "Got the Look" of a black dude, so he ain't "Free Fallin'" into a coma.

REPARATIONS ARTICLE 5H.
REVERSE LOUISIANA PURCHASE

White people, having worked very hard to retain the South during the Civil War and having used voter suppression and other tactics to retain power, shall be given the South—just not all the good parts—to do with as they wish. No federal funds (handouts) nor voting powers beyond local control shall be retained, to make sure that the South can credibly claim the right to say they are self-sufficient. Let them build pride in their work, allow them the dignity of work.

REPARATIONS ARTICLE 5I. WEED WHARTON

Upon ratification of this treaty, marijuana companies (weed businesses, marijuana holding companies, etc.) shall recruit their executives exclusively from the ranks of those incarcerated for doing an excellent job selling weed previously. This shall be the primary consideration for employment, not being in a hedge fund, investment partnership, management trust, or any other bullshit.

REPARATIONS ARTICLE 5J.
TAKE US INTO CUSTODY

Although black people shall endeavor to be blameless in all respects, on the occasion of a dispute wherein the police or other law enforcement shall be called to mediate, we require an expansion of our options. No longer shall police shoot first, having been "scared" or having "perceived a threat." Police shall be required to treat white and black suspects the same, with the option to "apprehend" or "take into custody."

REPARATIONS ARTICLE 5K.
THE WHITE CASTLE DOCTRINE

Due to the historic infiltration of law enforcement by racists and white supremacists, and in consideration of the fact that White Castle serves up food without calling anyone the N-word, we now require personnel decisions to be made by the White Castle human resources department, until such a time as racists are rooted out of the police, border security, and so on.

In the event of a dispute, White Castle HR can ask Taco Bell HR to arbitrate.

Reparations Article 5l. Stay Put

Whenever white people wander around, black and brown people die. Now that there are multiple streaming platforms, there's no need to go out quite so much. Stay home, enjoy a night in so that we may also enjoy a night in or out. White people, especially cops, are hereby ordered to stay in and binge-watch some of the new offerings on Apple TV+ or Hulu before they start going around exploring, and possibly killing.

Article VI: We Are Part of America

We're not going anywhere. As such, we demand full access to America, with full rights and privileges thereof. Furthermore:

Reparations Article 6a.
It's Curtains for Curtains

White people can have sheer curtains only. Full transparency means full transparency. Maybe you can have those beaded curtains. But no drapes. Venetian blinds are okay, as long as they are partway open. You can use shutters the same way, because we know you all love those. Wiping out prejudice and bias will take time, and until then we want to keep an eye on you all. Justice is blind. Justice has blinds.

Reparations Article 6b. Invisible Men

Henceforth there shall be inclusion and diversity in the realm of the imaginary, the made-up, and the fantastical. There are real black people and there shall thus be unreal black people. The world of make-believe, science fiction, fantasy, and any other genre of fancy, reverie, or invention shall be open to black imaginary people. This shall include but not be limited to imaginary friends, fictional characters, spies, phantoms, and ghosts.

Huh. You know, I look at all the proposals and I worry that it's still not gonna work. So let's just put it this way:

We want to be part of America. Maybe you still won't agree to giving us money, but if you agree that you won't kill us without anybody being brought to account, if you agree that you're not going to discriminate against us in your laws and practices, if you agree to come to terms with the history of this country and our shared place in it, and if you agree that you're not going to deny us a fair and equitable opportunity to a reasonable life, that would be a start. *Life, Liberty and the pursuit of Happiness,* right?

SIGNATURE PAGE

NOTE: Must be signed by all white people. Please pass along to your white friends like a chain letter. Oh, wait . . . did I say "chain"? My bad. We probably shouldn't be talking about chains at this time, but I'm just saying make sure everybody gets this thing. There's less and less white folks, but there's still a lot, so don't skip nobody.

Please sign below to agree to the treaty. I already added my John Hancock:

[signature: God Bless]

If you are unable to make it to the signing of our treaty at the Magic Johnson Theatre on the date the treaty is ratified, don't worry. You can still be a part of history by signing on to the pledge below!

INSTRUCTIONS:

1. Fill out the form below.

2. If you're black, no postage necessary. Doesn't it feel good to be the winner?

3. If you're white: Come on, man; after all this, you still want us to pay for your postage? You have the fucking money. Consider your stamp a down payment on your reparations.

CUT HERE
....

☑YES, I SURRENDER! I want to agree to the above terms and take responsibility for making the world a better place by acknowledging the wisdom and truth contained in this peace treaty.

☐ No, I am still in denial and don't wish to be part of the solution. I'd rather keep the systemic oppression, aggravation, and fading social status of white supremacy. In supplying my contact information, I acknowledge that any information provided may be used in further enforcement actions.

Name: Address: City, State, Zip Code:	To: I Surrender! P.O. Box 555 New York, NY 11111

ACKNOWLEDGMENTS

I want to thank my literary crew: my editor Peter Hubbard, my collaborator Doug Moe, and my agent Richard Abate. I'm grateful for my radio family: David Kantor, Skip Cheatham, and Jasmine Sanders. Thanks to Leyna Santos; Yvette Shearer; my Comedy Get Down brothers, Eddie Griffin, Cedric "The Entertainer," and George Lopez; my road team, Gary Monroe, Lew Oliver, and Derek Robles! Thanks also to my managers Michael Rotenberg and Dave Becky, my agent Nick Nuciforo, my dude Kensation Johnson, and my right-hand Sonya Vaughn. Thank you, Molly Gendell, Anwesha Basu, and Kayleigh George. Love to my family: my children, Ryan, Kyle, and Tyler, and my sexy-ass wife, LaDonna Hughley.